Thank you.

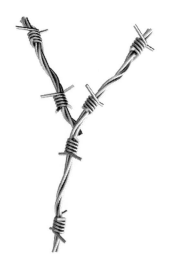

A HOLOCAUST MEMOIR

by
JACK ADLER
with
W.F. ASPENWALL

MBEDZI PUBLISHING

2012

For information address Mbedzi Publishing,

6119 Greenville Ave. 162, Dallas, Texas 75206-1906 USA

www.mbedzipublishing.com

ISBN 13:978-0-9849842-3-7

ISBN 10:0-9849842-3-2

Book packaging and design by Jacqui Terry,

www.jacquiterry.com Kitchener, Ontario, CANADA

Edited by Elizabeth Humphrey,

www.bookwormediting.com Bookworm Editing, Denver, Colorado USA

Cover Art by Morgan Cook, Golden, Colorado USA

Library of Congress Control Number: 2012931615

FIRST EDITION

April 19, 2012

MBEDZI PUBLISHING

To my family who perished in the Holocaust.

My father Cemach E. Adler, age 45,

in the Kaufering Concentration Camp

My mother Fella R. Adler, age 42, in the Pabianice Ghetto

My brother Chaim U. Adler, age 18, in the Pabianice Ghetto

My sister Ester Adler, age 19,

in the Bergen-Belsen Concentration Camp

My sister Peska I. Adler, age 12,

in the Auschwitz/Birkenau Gas Chamber

&

To my wonderful children and grandchildren…my Miracle Family.

My son Elliott C. Adler and his wife Laura

My granddaughter Lauren Adler

My grandson Matthew Adler

My daughter Paula F. Shapiro and her husband Les

My grandson Jessie Shapiro

My grandson Cary Shapiro

A special dedication to my Lifetime Partner.

Judy K. Segal

THIS BOOK IS a narrative and should be read as such. All events in this novel have been recorded to the best of my memory. I ask my readers to always question; if a statistic or detail seems inaccurate at any level, research, read, and question.

The truth is often shocking. Be mindful, my friend.

Ask Y.

JACK ADLER

PREFACE

IT DIDN'T TAKE long for me to decide on a title for my book. I've known it for years, in fact—knew that if I ever wrote this, I would call it "Y". Understanding the institution of hate is a demanding task. How can one even begin to comprehend such a thing? Hate breeds everywhere and is the product of man. I want to understand; this is my endeavor. So, I ask. Why?

Why do we hate? Why do we worship the differences among men and ignore those things that make us one? Why do we both as victims and perpetrators fall prey to pressures of hate? Why do we let religion and other institutions and belief systems divide us so decisively? The answers are not simple. They are not clear. I still cannot help but to ask…why?

History teaches us that questioning is itself the point. Why remember history if not to question the causes, the outcomes, and the men and women who committed acts of the most acute kindness and of the most horrible evils? We must learn. We must teach. We must adhere to the principles of the Golden Rule.

Treat others as we ourselves want to be treated.

So why don't we? Why don't we attempt to be free of hate? And if we do, what more can be done in the effort? Why don't we do more?

I ask you, the reader…why? Y?

The letter "Y" has become symbolic of the word in this world of technology and simplicity. I embrace the letter as a means to simplify the question itself. We need to ask this question more than we do, more than we have.

"Y" was once called "waw", its language of heritage belonging to the early Hebrew people, a heritage I share.

But I am not writing this to teach you about the origins of the alphabet or even to delve into the annals of history more than I've already done in this book. I am writing because I want you to ask. I need you to ask.

Y?

JACK ADLER, 2012

FOREWORD

JACK'S A FUNNY GUY. I didn't expect this to be my first impression of an eighty-three-year-old Holocaust survivor, with whom I would eventually have some of the most serious and dramatic conversations of my life.

When I met him for the first time after we decided to work together on this book, he opened with a joke.

"You mentioned during our last conversation that you breed dogs," he started. Knowing full well already any breed-specific information I had given him, he continued. "What kind of dogs?" His eyes were inquisitive and honest.

"German Shepherds," I said, trying to answer quickly, but with a budding curiosity of my own. I knew he already knew this, but I was also aware Jack was a jokester and wanted to see where his question would go. I had an inclination that it would have something to do with the German-Jew association.

"I, too, had a German Shepherd once. It found out I was Jewish and bit me," he said with emphasis on the punch line. I could tell immediately that he meant the joke with nothing but full amusement, no amount of grudge in his voice concerning Germans...or dogs for that matter. Later I found out that he did indeed get bitten by a German Shepherd. He was marching in line outside of Dachau when he drifted just a bit and the well-trained canine bit him without a moment of provocation on Jack's part. He just *stepped* wrong.

These stories piled in my notes, moments of tense sorrow, fear-inspiring torture, and pitiful excuses for the human experience.

But with each story told, about memories the likes of which those who've come since can only imagine with gritted sympathy, came a joke meant to lighten the mood and bring a smile to a face on the verge of tears.

On one such occurrence we were engaged in a discussion about Jack's time in one of the concentration camps in Kaufering, Germany. My voice recorder was ticking away the seconds and minutes. As he was relaying his tale of the last time he spoke to his father, I jotted in shorthand about some writing ideas that I would reexamine when I transcribed the audio. I stopped writing and looked up, ready to ask one of my many interrupting questions.

"Tell me, Jack, did you learn a lot of languages during your experience? I know enough of the history of these places to know there were many languages in each camp. You might talk to your father in one language, a fellow prisoner in another, and yet of course need to know German," I said, realizing I spoke the obvious and thinking maybe the question was rather silly.

"Indeed, young man," he began, "you would be surprised at how quickly one can learn a language when one must." He paused thoughtfully and regarded me with half-closed eyes. He continued after a few breaths. "Would you believe it, I learned every language but Greek." His tone was flat and even.

I couldn't sense a joke from his manner of expression, but it was obvious he was kidding. I walked into it anyway, a broad smile spilling across my face. "Say something in Chinese, then," I said.

"Sorry, that's Greek to me."

That's Jack. A multi-faceted man of eighty-three years who saw undeniable prejudice and anti-Semitism in his boyhood home of Poland, who witnessed the atrocities and horrors of years spent in a pair of ghettos and three concentration camps thereafter, who did his stint in the U.S. Army, the very entity that helped him to realize liberation—and who has spent years since raising a family and speaking to millions about his intimacies with the faces of hatred. Somehow, though, he has retained that glimpse into the humorous, a zeal to find and maintain happiness, and an active optimism focused on the ideal of human goodness. He knows we are capable of more than we are or demonstrate, and his goal to share this wisdom comes with a humility to which I can only aspire.

I am humbled, though, by the utter privilege of helping Jack tell his tale. Be aware, however, that all the elements of memoir and message are his own. I was able to provide the syntax, the punctuation, and once every so often, the diction. Any errors therein are my own.

During our time together, Jack was a mentor. His philosophies and ideas on religion, culture—humanity in general—were not taboo. He answered every question and willingly shared those very things. As I still reach to become the man I hope to be, Jack's time with me only facilitated that process. I'm a better man because of Jack Adler.

There aren't many people I have met in my travels and experiences that have done this (or been that) for me.

I hope I get to hear many more of Jack's jokes, to share more with him, and to understand the world a little more each time I'm in his presence. But, in the meantime, I am excited and proud to know that this is now in print, that this (his story) can be shared with more than just me. I'm selfish sometimes, and think we all are on occasion. But now is not a time for selfishness.

My time with Jack is not my own. It's far too valuable.

I hope you get as much from reading "Y" as I did working with Jack and striking each key to record this forever. I challenge you upon completion to take Jack's own adage to heart:

"Don't bite the bait that leads to hate."

What can you do to make your world, our world, a better place? A place free of the hatred that so many had to endure.

I would like to leave you with a message of "happy reading", but I can't. The glimpses into Jack's memory penned here are not happy ones. But I promise to tell you more of Jack's jokes, and to help you find the smile that holds back the tears as you come to the absolute realization that hatred isn't a requirement of humanity.

W.F. ASPENWALL, 2012

PART I

INTRODUCTION

MY BUTTONS

MEMOIRS ARE OFTEN incomplete. They relive recollections (some good, some bad) that often lack a context for the tale. I don't want my story to be among those. I want my story to be a focal point that illustrates a greater message.

Many Holocaust survivors have penned narratives. These memoirs run the range, like all literature, from good to bad, meaningful to lacking purpose outside of simple expression of experience (and there is nothing wrong with that). But what they all have in common is the absolute necessity to share—and in sharing, allowing readers to learn and remember. For what would be the consequence if we forgot?

I don't want to *just* tell my story, as I am only one of millions of members of a community who witnessed the worst of humanity. My story is like each of theirs, no different. I lived. I experienced. I witnessed. I survived. There are six million more who cannot share their story. They were erased. We attempt to remember for them, but their stories will never be told. I do not represent anything special beyond the scope of just one more voice that finally found a page.

But…a glimpse for a moment into my boyhood. My own first experiences with anti-Semitism are among my earliest memories. I was just a boy, just beginning to know the world with the developing cognition of youth—a time to which we can all trace our first remembered events. I am old now, but unfortunately, hatred is much harder to forget than some levels of happiness.

I was outside of a Catholic church on a Sunday morning in Pabianice, a small city in the Lodz area of Poland. I lived at number 41 Ulica Warszawska (Warsaw Street). It's funny what I can remember. But I can't remember what brought me near the church at that time—maybe I was playing with friends. My mother used to tell me not to go near the entrance of the church on

Sundays or during Christian holidays, but I didn't listen. I was so inquisitive then. So I disobeyed. It doesn't matter, though. I was outside the church when the families began to file out after morning mass. I often walked past the church, and never thought too much of it.

I remember the boys. I thought they were my friends, but the reality of the situation was that our friendship in youth was coming to a close as they learned to hate. They learned this hatred from their parents, their church, and even their school, and it was as sociably acceptable as any ordinary act. One of the boys took notice of me first. I thought he would say hello; he did not. He was only a few years older than me. He was dressed in his best, pressed clothes, and he wore a broad smile that stretched from ear to ear under a spread of dirty blond hair. He was just a normal boy, nothing otherwise special about his appearance or demeanor. That his behavior to follow was also considered normal is perhaps the most shocking, and difficult thing to comprehend.

The slurs came first. When he saw me and recognized me, knowing full well I was Jewish, the filth that spilled from his mouth is something I am glad I cannot remember—as I wouldn't even want to speak it. Suffice it to say, the remarks were born of evil and represented the culturally acceptable hatred that was infused into my hometown. He shouted dirty epithets for Jew and pointed at me with a slim, accusing finger. I looked around. He must be talking to someone else, I thought. But I was the only one in front of him. He came up to me and I tensed.

I was wearing a wonderfully fashionable jacket. It had bright, beautiful buttons that glowed with gleaming brilliance in the morning sun. The boy reached for the top one first. He wrapped his delicate fingers around it and yanked, tearing the fabric and freeing the button. He tossed it to the dusty street, that smile still painted across his face.

I looked down, but couldn't comprehend what had just happened. I was in shock as much as if I had just broken a bone. He sought the next button down, and I couldn't move. I was frozen with something akin to fear or surprise—a combination of both is possible, I think. He tore that button, too, and then continued to liberate me of each until they all rested on the ground near my feet. They immediately looked dull and very unlike the buttons in which I once had pride in possessing.

The boy laughed and turned to his parents who were nearby, as well as a few other adult onlookers from inside the church. I don't know what I expected, but I can imagine that I waited for them to berate their son for his rude actions and physically demeaning abuse. Instead, I discovered his smile was inherited. His parents grinned, if only for a moment, then took his hand and turned their backs. I was a forgotten entity—as if I had only provided a brief moment of humor on their pleasant Sunday afternoon.

I gathered the buttons and took them home. Confused.

My first acquaintance with anti-Semitism was mild in comparison to many others. Some grew up in slavery. Others died as infants, tossed into fires or used as target practice. Many didn't taste the bitterness of this evil until a ride on a cattle car, torture at the hands of those with different views from their own, or the slow, painful death realized in a gas chamber.

I lost my buttons.

But there would be worse to come.

PART II

THE NARRATIVE OF THE LIFE
OF YACOB SZLAMEK ADLER

My Life Before the Holocaust

My grandfather, and most of his ten children including my father, worked in the textile industry in Pabianice and Lodz. During the weekdays my father would travel to and from Lodz on a street car. When he returned, he used to bring home freshly cut kosher salami. I loved it. It was on such a day, hours before my father was to return, I was climbing trees when I should have been somewhere else.

I used to play hooky from school. I was an inquisitive boy—so inquisitive in fact that I wondered if there wasn't more to learn outside in the trees than in school. I spoke both Polish and Yiddish and attended public and Hebrew schools alike. But I liked to be absent; I was restless, young, and endlessly curious. A spot of preference during a typical skipping session was the small orchard behind the apartment building where we lived. My grandfather owned the property, so I felt no remorse about climbing the stunted fruit trees that grew there.

Apple and cherry trees were my playground, and occasionally my sustenance. My family, more preoccupied with adult matters, didn't notice or didn't care to mention they noticed that I would enjoy my time in the trees when I was supposed to be tending to my studies instead.

Sometimes a friend or two would join me and we would swing from branch to branch, destroying blossoms, with little care about the adult world—a world on the brink of war that was the whisper of old men and the debate of our educated fathers. There were hints of what was to come, but nothing concerning to a ten-year-old boy at play.

At Number 41 Ulica Warszawska in Pabianice, Poland, my life was school, temple, tree branches, and friends—the common practices of a young man with concerns that ranged from toys to candy to smiles. It was on such a day of skipping my classes when I was introduced—with full force—to the world of Nazis and war.

OUR APARTMENT BUILDING was on one of the main streets that ran through the very heart of Pabianice. (In April of 2011, I visited this place. It looks much the same as I remember, but now belongs to someone else. What should be family property is instead a real estate investment for someone I will never meet.) From the confines of the orchard, I heard the rumbling of engines and people cheering. I didn't know of any parade that was supposed to take place, but my curiosity was piqued.

I gripped a broad branch and swung myself down, flipping feet over head until I landed like a professional acrobat on the hard earth beneath. I was alone that day. I stood still for a moment, trying to listen and identify the commotion that came from the other side of the buildings. The rumbles became roars and the cheering intensified. I sprinted through the yard and around the corner, dirt and twigs in my hair no doubt, not one to miss whatever exciting event was transpiring.

I wasn't the only child playing hooky that day. Dozens of kids, many I knew, stood along either side of the street. Most were with their families, held in the proud embraces of parents eager to raise their hands in celebration. They all looked so happy—so relieved.

On the first week of September, 1939, the Nazis arrived in our city.

Several military transport vehicles adorned with painted eagles and flags bearing the swastika bore through the center of the street like a burrowing snake. I did not know at whom or what I was looking, but I was impressed. Each of the trucks was awe-inspiring—all angles and precision—and carried smiling soldiers who wore guns over their shoulders and raised their hands in odd salutes. They looked clean, happy, and proud. It was like a party of some kind; nothing this grand ever happened in our town—I must have missed the invitation.

It must be noted that German anti-Semitism and Polish anti-Semitism were a far cry from one another, different breeds of the same species of hatred. Many Poles hated Jews, but more Germans hated Jews—to death. In fact, the Germans and the Poles had their own conflicts, and in most places in Poland, the Nazis were not welcomed with open arms. Pabianice was different, but

I don't know why. Perhaps the Poles feared the soldiers, and thus wanted to appear to welcome them so. As a boy, thoughts like these were far from my mind, and I only knew that our town was happy and the atmosphere exciting, be it a guise or no.

Some of the women approached the slow moving caravan; they were adorned with bright lipstick and freshly curled hair. They covered their mouths in joy and handed the soldiers colorful bouquets. Others threw their flowers and gifts at the young men in uniform while shouting messages of thanks and praise.

My classmates' fathers shook hands with the nearest soldiers, welcoming them to our town with all the zeal of those moved by a religious experience, their eyes glazed over with an emotion I couldn't identify.

I didn't know *not* to clap with the others. More likely than not, I would have been ostracized had I dared refrain from conformity. I joined in, but spent most of my time pushing to the front to get a better look. I found my way between two overweight older women I didn't know. I squeezed between their hips and, at the front, I could see much better.

Black bent crosses against seas of red were not only on the flags that fluttered in the wind behind each transport; the men with the guns sitting shoulder to shoulder wore a patch with the same design on their upper arms. It was almost…pretty. I never could have imagined, with the mind of the innocent child, that the symbol and colors I regarded would become the epitome of evil and hatred all over the world. Only too soon would I become achingly familiar with the mark.

Again, the stiff arm salute. Some in the crowd mimicked the gesture, but I refrained.

I was only ten years old.

Not even in my wildest imagination could I have envisioned what those men had in store for us—the very evil that was our fate. But I didn't have to wait long. I ran home after the Germans passed, eager to tell my parents what I saw.

AT THE TIME, my immediate family numbered six—my parents, Cemach and Fella; my brother, Chaim; two sisters, Ester and Peska; and myself. I also had a very large extended family, eighty-three individuals including grandparents, aunts, uncles, and cousins. Beginning immediately with the Nazi occupation, that number began to diminish dramatically over the course of several years that witnessed occupation, two ghettos, more concentration camps, and liberation for only a few.

WITHIN JUST A few hours of the formal procession down our city streets, notices were posted throughout the city. The Nazis hung them on church and temple doors, schools, places of commerce, and anywhere people would be likely to see them right away. These notices concerned the Jewish population of Pabianice. There were just over eight thousand of us that day in 1939.

These notices were simple and direct. My father was the first to see one and tell us what they said.

He recited, "Effective immediately, no person of Jewish descent is allowed to be outdoors unless he or she wears two yellow Stars of David attached visibly to the clothing. One star must be worn on the front, the other on the back."

We stared at him with little comprehension. It almost seemed like a silly request from such formal men as those I had seen ride through the street with such pride and good-natured expressions.

We thought he was done, but he continued.

"Effective immediately, no Jewish child may attend any public school in Poland. Effective immediately, all Jewish places of worship are closed and Jews are forbidden to meet in these places or practice religion." His voice was stern and we all understood how serious these last two mandates were. Looking back now, I am curious as to what our father saw in his children's eyes.

I couldn't understand, though I tried, how or why they would keep us out of school or from going to temple. I had no great love for either, but as soon as someone tells another what he cannot do, that removal and denial of freedom comes as a shocking assault.

We stared at my father with wide eyes and gaping mouths. The rest of the conversation that night was one of somber and morose reality. My youngest sister and I knew very little about what was going on, but our father warned us about the serious nature of what would soon transpire.

"Obey the soldiers," he told us. "Stay away from them if you can." He was gentle with us, but he was masking a growing anger for which he would never have or be allowed an outlet.

We nodded without asking why this time.

THINGS CHANGED DRAMATICALLY and quickly. It began with the destruction of our local synagogue. It was only days after the arrival of the Nazi occupiers. Our neighbors, people we trusted and knew well, were among the masses that stormed into our temple and stripped it completely of its interior. We had no say in the matter. Furniture, religious relics and texts—everything was destroyed or looted. The local population burned those things they removed. Torahs became black smoke that drifted skyward in lazy swirls. Within hours the building had become a stable for horses.

The entire building was eventually demolished by the Germans during the war.

I didn't miss the synagogue necessarily, but I saw the symbolic destruction in the eyes of my parents and other adults in our Jewish community. Some shed tears that lasted days, a bit of their souls leaking out with each reluctant drop.

When one group of people denies another group of people the freedom of religious practice, this only shows how religion—whether Christianity, Judaism, or any other—can be used as a tool for hatred. The Nazis used their own version of Christian values to deny our practice. Unfortunately, this is not the first time in history and most assuredly is not the last time this would be allowed to happen. Organized religion, when used as a means to hate and kill, is the most dangerous weapon in the world.

THE PHYSICAL ABUSE against the Jewish people began after the limitations of freedom and the destruction of our properties. Beatings and murder were as frequent as breathing. At random, and without notice, Nazi soldiers entered various Jewish neighborhoods to wreak the havoc that became our version of normal.

Once there, they would select men and women. If the selected individuals ran, the Nazis chased them as if they were animals. They used whips and trained attack dogs to force the unfortunate people into the town square, where they were then publicly beaten and humiliated. The place I used to play games with friends became a place the Nazis would strike a woman, a child, or the elderly full-force and with no remorse. It became a place where they would whip our fathers until they were bloodied and unconscious. It became a place where they would cut our hair for fun and shout slurs that were soon picked up and shared by people who stood by and watched it all happen. Young Jewish men and women were flogged mercilessly for failure to salute the Nazi flag, the flag of our oppressors.

I was near the square during a similar demonstration of this horrible violence. I heard shouting and screaming from the center, and a crowd surrounded the area as if they were watching a street performer. I couldn't see what was happening, but I heard the pleas of the beaten. A man begged for the soldier to stop, for the soldier to have mercy. His screams were like ice picks in my ears, but most of the crowd seemed wholly unconcerned. Some looked on in fascination—both horrified and amused...a performance to their liking. A soldier spoke words in German that I couldn't understand. They were brief.

Then a gunshot echoed.

It was deafening and blasted the square with a wave of shock that resonated among us. People began walking away in silence. I didn't see it happen, but I saw the aftermath. I didn't recognize the man who was left in the square after the Nazi soldier nonchalantly holstered his gun and left as though he had been at target practice.

There was nothing left of the man for me to recognize; the man could have been family or friend, I will never know. He had been shot point-blank and was face down in a pool of bright crimson that contrasted with the dark stone and quickly spread across the ground around him. I don't know how long I was there. It could have been minutes or hours. I couldn't tear myself away at first, thrown headfirst into the grim nature of our new condition. I didn't cry or shake. Eventually, I turned around and went home.

I couldn't bring myself to tell my family what had happened.

Events like that also became normal. If a Jew protested against treatment, that Jew was shot on the spot. There was no forum for political or religious rights, no police or military to protect us. Immediately and without justification, we were no longer men. If anyone objected to his treatment, he was shot.

These daily expressions of evil continued for a couple of months before the soldiers moved the Jewish population of Pabianice into a ghetto. For those months, that near ritualistic form of torture and oppression was accepted. The Nazis enforced and accepted it. The locals accepted it. Even we accepted it.

What else could we do?

The Ghetto in Pabianice, Poland

Our ghetto was an open area in one of the oldest parts of Pabianice, a city steeped in history, old buildings, and tradition. It was actually called Old Town. The fact that it was open meant that there were no fences, barbed wire, or other deterrents surrounding us and keeping us in. Our barbed wire was psychological. It was the guns the soldiers carried, their willingness to kill, and the hopelessness that already afflicted us like a disease. They didn't need a fence to keep us in.

We were too scared to leave.

Old Town had previously been home to Christians and Jews alike, but as a section of this quaint part of town was established as our official and secluded housing sector, the Christian inhabitants had to leave. The government took care of them, however. They moved into nicer parts of Pabianice, some gaining possession and moving into the homes and apartments of former Jewish residents who themselves were forced to relocate to the ghetto.

The buildings in this area were older than others, host to climbing vines, crumbling masonry, and cracked windowpanes. Our entire family was forced to live in one room. Others were made to live the same way, and thus we found ourselves without privacy and without space.

The Nazis gave us a very strict curfew, and we had to obey. We did so without question, making sure not to leave our designated areas except when we were allowed, usually for work or during daylight hours. But without school, temple, and humanity, there was little cause to leave anyway. We spent our time talking, sharing rumors, and hoping for an end we all promised ourselves would come soon.

There were other rules as well, rules that transformed us into cattle. The ghetto in Pabianice was split in half, a main street dividing it. We were only allowed to move between buildings during the daylight hours and only then to cross the street twice a day, once in the morning and once in the late afternoon. The Nazis tracked our movement and kept close watch on us. All the while, the beatings and shootings continued.

It became habit to look for soldiers in all directions before moving at all. As shadows of humanity, we clung to corners, alleys, and darkness for safety.

WE ALSO BECAME slaves.

The Nazis formed a Jewish committee in the ghetto, but this was not a committee formed to represent the people there to any degree. The committee's primary function was to provide the Nazis with a list of names for slave labor to work outside the ghetto. The work varied from construction to baking to other more militaristic pursuits that could serve the war effort.

But it wasn't always the committee's task to name and secure workers. Often, Nazi soldiers would barge in through our doors and take people away for whatever job needed doing. These intrusions into our lives were always abrupt and violent, but—after a while—never a surprise. I was still a little too young for work and my brother was already becoming sickly. It was my father who had the most to fear from these spontaneous visits to procure slave laborers.

I was beginning to understand the twisted nature of our condition, at least to the degree that a child's mind could comprehend. I understood we were hated and that we were considered something less than human. Contact with us was to be avoided if possible. Thus, I remember vividly the moment I devised a plan to hide my father from such visits.

I could hear the soldiers pushing through a door not far from our own. They barked orders at the inhabitants they found there and, because of the routine, I knew they would soon repeat the process and come for my father. I had to do something.

My father wasn't one to harbor fear, at least not in our eyes, but even my little sister Peska could tell he was worried the soldiers would enter our room and take him away, perhaps for a few hours, perhaps forever.

I looked around at our meager accommodations to find something, anything, for escape. It was our clothes hamper that provided such a refuge. The hamper was tall and wide and could easily hold a grown man. I ran without thinking as we heard the soldiers move another door closer to ours, demanding other able-bodied men to come with them. When I arrived at the lip of the hamper, I called to my father as I began pulling various articles of clothing from the hamper's depth, cradling them in my arms in a haphazard bundle.

"Get in," I said to him. His gaze was sad and searching. His youngest son was trying to save him. How could he argue? It was like I was the father and he was the son.

We stood staring at each other in silence for a few more long seconds, the echoes of footfalls drawing near. I'm sure if I had concentrated I could have heard the soldiers' breath strike our door just moments before they were to enter.

"Make sure the clothes cover me completely and tell Peska to keep quiet and not to look to me when they come," he said, becoming my father again. His strong brown eyes never wavered as he ran his hand through his already graying hair with an exaggerated release of breath. He swung a leg over the edge of the hamper and contorted his body until he was squatting as low as he could manage.

Just as I was blanketing him with the last item, an old, soiled pair of pants, the footsteps stopped at our door. I rushed to Peska's side, nearly out of breath—not from exertion but from worry and doubt in my efforts. I held her hand—our fingers interlocking—and faced the door just as it swung open with a rush of air and slammed against the wall. Two soldiers entered carrying guns they wore strapped around their necks. Their fingers rested on triggers and their demeanor lacked any compassion.

Around them I could just make out a short line of men I recognized from town, Jews who were living in the building with us. They had been selected and were waiting for assignments. The soldiers both started to speak in German as they walked through our apartment looking for adult men.

I couldn't understand them until one finally spoke in Polish. "Where is your father?"

I shook my head and squeezed Peska's hand as the muzzle of his gun came level with my head. My mother and brother entered from a side room, walking slowly arm-in-arm, eyes downcast. They made for a pitiful sight and were nothing of interest to the soldiers who, luckily enough, were in a hurry to move to the next family, then the next, and be on about their business.

I had forgotten to tell Peska not to look at the hamper; I hadn't had time. I cringed when she did. It must have gone unnoticed, but for a brief instant I imagined the men opening fire on the container and my father within. But, it was of no concern to them if they even looked that way. Why would they want to poke through the dirty clothes of a dirtier people? They began speaking again and one laughed as he looked at my mother.

We waited until long after they left to dare move. Maybe a half hour passed before we finally approached the hamper and removed the scarce camouflage I had provided my father. He stood and winced because of the cramps in his legs, and gently removed himself from his sanctuary.

It would not be the last time one of us would hide him in such a way. As much as anything else, this became our practice—our tradition. The committee could not protect him, and perhaps some might have seen our actions as unfair, but we loved and protected our father—a man whose strength, faith, and resilience were dedicated to loving and protecting us.

ASIDE FROM THE responsibility to offer up laborers, the committee also distributed food to the residents in equal and meager portions, just enough to keep the "animals" alive.

I had eaten well my whole life up until the ghetto; I had enjoyed delicacies without remorse and extra portions with no added thought or concern for gluttony.

They gave us our rations. One slice of bread. One bowl of soup. This was our daily allowance. Sometimes the batter for the bread was supplemented with sawdust if supplies were low. I would eat little else until my liberation so many years later. I weighed more as a ten-year-old boy than when my liberating saviors rescued me at seventeen.

We began to starve. At first, when one experiences hunger, he has the feeling that he is not eating as much as he once did. The stomach aches and dizziness, nausea, and other feelings dominate his physical presence. But the human body is fairly resilient. One can grow accustomed to some of the worst conditions possible. We did. We became accustomed to the singular piece of bread and the small bowl of soup.

When we could, we ate something to supplement our rations. People traded, people searched, and people begged. Sometimes, the result was a little something extra. Sometimes, the result was death for the effort.

My mother once had to try.

My older brother Chaim became very sick and his condition worsened due to the enforced malnutrition. He needed more food to fight fever—more to survive. At one point, he had been the strongest among us, a boy on the verge of manhood. He was reduced to a mere fraction of what he had been—and in short time. We did what we could for him, but with no real access to medicines and no way to give him more of what he needed, we watched him drift slowly away.

My mother would have none of it.

She left our crowded quarters one evening without permission and under the cover of darkness, risking her life to help Chaim. She snuck out of the ghetto and past soldiers when they turned their backs, clinging to the shadows as if they were a veil of protection.

She went from home to home, visiting the residences of people we once called friends. She begged for anything they might offer—anything extra that might help her son live. Some apologized, some slammed doors, and others ignored her with stares full of indifference.

She came to a final home. The woman who lived there had been very close to my mother, and Mother hoped her pleas would not fall on deaf ears for the last time before she retreated back to her family. She knocked softly, not wishing to alarm anyone inside. She must have already felt the defeat creep upon her. Any local who helped a Jew in such a manner could be punished just as easily by the German occupiers. But she dared one more time.

The door opened slowly, and only a crack, as my mother's Polish friend peered through to see who was there, as though wary of the dark and what it might bring.

"Please, Chaim is so very sick," my mother began, before the woman interrupted her.

"Go away, Fella. You shouldn't be here."

My mother could not be told no again. "Please…he's so ill, we only need a little. Anything. Can you please help? Do you have any food you can give me to take to him?" I only heard this story second-hand, but I am positive my mother's voice was desperate. Had she been overheard by anyone else, she probably would have died right there, killed at the doorstep of an old friend.

The woman paused and looked at my mother with perhaps a sympathetic pain. "Wait here," she said before disappearing and shutting the door behind her.

Maybe my mother said a silent prayer. Or maybe she was afraid her friend was off telling her husband.

She waited.

Finally, the woman opened the door again, just a sliver—large enough to reach her hand through. My mother's hands came up to collect whatever was offered. The woman placed one egg in those begging, trembling hands. The door shut at once and all was silent.

One egg. My mother risked her life, perhaps all our lives, for one egg for my sick brother. She returned home with her prize and told us what happened while preparing it for Chaim. He ate quietly and could barely keep it down.

I WISH THAT was the last memory of my mother, but it is not. I remember her death with all the reality of yesterday.

Chaim died first and with little event. I didn't guess his fate or even imagine death was a possibility. He became ill, one night fell asleep, and when we woke in the morning, he was no longer breathing. He looked like a painted, peaceful version of himself. The shock of his passing was what made it bearable. I don't remember crying, but I remember missing him. Though big brothers and little brothers often have their conflicts, he was a pillar of familiarity and love I miss still today. He was my brother…and the first to die in my immediate family.

Chaim's death only quickened my mother's. Weeks passed as she transformed.

I remember her black, wavy hair pressed in damp curls over her forehead as my father touched a damp rag against her skin. She didn't register his efforts, but simply let her half-closed eyes drift to each of us in turn.

She had become a frail shell of the beautiful woman she had been, but her hazel eyes were still so gripping when she finally let them come to rest on me. I didn't know how to feel; I was sad for her suffering, but couldn't comprehend that if those eyes shut, they would not open again. In thinking about the moment, I think she knew and she understood. She kept them open as long as she could.

Like my brother, her condition had deteriorated. The soup and bread was just not enough to sustain her. And when she became sick and needed more, there were no more eggs to be begged from a neighbor. I watched my mother become a skeletal shadow of humanity. A wraith of an oppressed people. The process was slow and painful. First, she could no longer keep her head up, and then she could no longer walk without great effort and dizziness. Bedridden in her last days, she tried to speak to us with the optimism only a mother can manage.

"Everything will be fine, my children," she would say. "I will get better. Mother is just sick."

I wanted so badly to believe her. I was old enough that I didn't.

To each of my two sisters, Mother's eyes turned and absorbed. Peska was crying already and Ester's face had become puffy and swollen. She was on the verge of a breakdown. When my mother's eyes looked to me, I lost myself in them, free from death and worry. The solace in our locked gaze was a miracle to which I wanted so desperately to cling. But it was not lasting. Her eyes left me and found my father.

They held there so long. One tear trailed down my father's face and was lost in the short black beard he wore before the camps.

Mother closed her eyes for the last time at exactly ten o'clock that Thursday night, her last night.

Later, assigned workers came for my mother's body. We huddled together that evening, my sisters crying. Father was beyond tears and just held the girls. I walked around the room until I could no longer manage the sound of their cries anymore, went to bed, and fell asleep with the vision of my mother's eyes.

BOTH MY MOTHER, Fella Adler, and my brother, Chaim Adler, died of malnutrition and related illnesses while in the ghetto of Pabianice. They were buried in graves with no markers. The only consolation I have is that they never had to see the worst of what happened to our family—to our people.

(I visited the cemetery in Pabianice in April of 2011, my first return since boyhood. I could not find their graves.)

THE FIRST LIQUIDATION

WE LIVED LIKE that in Pabianice until May 16, 1942, when the Germans finally notified us our ghetto would soon be liquidated. They would move the remainder of our population to undisclosed locations outside of the city, beginning by dividing us into two groups they labeled A and B. It seems odd that people could be treated in such a systematic and calculated manner, but much of the next few years for me and others would be similar divisions, lines, and groups—processes used to further strip us of our humanity. It was an assembly line of sorrow and death.

Everything was so precise it is hard to forget even the minute details. They told us to form these groups in front of our buildings at exactly two p.m. sharp. At two, Nazi officers and soldiers arrived and, with their guns up and attack dogs at their sides, marched us quickly to the nearby Krusz-Ender soccer field. The field was already divided, a clear line drawn right down the middle in the grass and dirt.

They shouted in German, which some of our group understood; the rest just followed the others. "Group A to the left, Group B to the right. Hurry!" More men shouted and dogs barked. Most of us were silent as we shuffled within the crowd to get to where the soldiers told us we belonged. It didn't take us long to realize the nature of our division. They had provided each of us an A or B label days before, but there hadn't been much discussion on the matter.

Group A consisted of the old, the young, and the sick or injured. Group B hosted those men and women who were deemed able-bodied enough to perform slave labor. I would see many separations like this in my near future.

I was crushed into my father's side, and with Chaim already gone, it was just the two of us and my older sister. I noticed with a start that little Peska was missing. I looked everywhere I could within the confines of our group, but could not find her. I was afraid and began to cry, but kept looking. It was my father who told us the reality: Peska was not in our group. She was in Group A with the elderly and the infirm. She was nine and a half years old at the time and must have been terrified without her family.

We waited for what seemed beyond eternity. For five hours we were made to stand on the field in those groups, clinging to the hope we would soon rest, soon eat. For their entertainment, the Nazis had Jews box one another or had the whole lot of us sing hate songs against our own religion and people. I wonder if the adults knew with any certainty what would happen to one group and what would happen to the other. At seven p.m. it was already quite dark and hard to see anyone not directly within arm's reach. Military vehicles swarmed around us and only then would we see more, aided by the headlights from the trucks. In that light, we saw them begin to move people out of Group A.

We worried for Peska, but were helpless. If my father had protested, or made to collect her from the other side, they would have killed him as surely as they were going to kill her, anyway.

Perhaps an hour after the soldiers began moving members of Group A off the field, they asked for volunteers from the B side where I waited in silence with my father and older sister. The Nazis needed people to pick up the debris left behind—articles of clothing, scraps of paper, and other items.

I hoped with an eager anxiety to see my sister again, so I was among the first to volunteer. They gave each of us a baby carriage; it is disgusting to even think why they had so many empty ones available. The carriages in those days were broad and deep, and they told us to use them as waste bins.

Darkness was my shield and savior that night.

I slowly moved around the other side of the field, bending over whenever I came across a wayward jacket or someone's papers. I didn't want to attract the attention of any of the remaining members of Group A, so I was quiet as a whisper while tending to my duty. Some of the trucks began to drive away—their headlights with them, and the scene became even more enveloped in the blackness of night. I got closer to the members of Group

A, but only a step at a time, careful not to stand out or give any reason to draw the ire or suspicion of the Nazi soldiers who stood in various positions around us. They were fewer now, but still present and watchful. The wheels of the carriage squealed and I winced each time the sound echoed into the night.

I finally dared to allow my sister's name to escape my lips, but only when I was nearly on top of the people who remained in A.

"Peska," I whispered. My eyes searched in the darkness, moving from the shadowy form of one person to the next, hoping to match her height with one of those apparitions. They all looked the same in the shroud of night.

"Peska," I risked again. The result was a sea of murmurs. Members of A began to take up her name and release it again like the ebbing of waves against a quiet shore. Her name sounded different on their lips, a reminder that things were not and never would again be as they were.

The wave of A pushed her forward like driftwood when they found her. I was in shock to see her appear out of the folds of darkness. She was terrified, shaking and crying in a low sob. She looked so frail and small.

"Don't stand still, Peska. Move back and forth to stay warm," I said, hoping somehow to help my sister. She complied.

Lights from a turning Nazi transport lit the group for a few seconds, and I froze. As it moved on, I bent at the waist, pretending to pick up a piece of paper that wasn't there. I wondered how many eyes were following my movement and if they would realize what I was doing. Would they (could they) know I wanted to save my sister? Could those beams from the truck lamps pierce right into my soul and reveal my intentions? I shivered involuntarily and the lights continued in their arch and then out into the distance.

"Wait for the lights, Peska. If it stays dark, get in the carriage," I said. It was barely audible, but she nodded that she understood and continued to sway.

No more lights passed for several minutes. I gestured to the carriage, and Peska climbed in as quickly as she could. Even at nine years old, she was still quite small and fit perfectly in the depths of the carriage when she curled into a ball. I immediately began to push away from the group, angling toward B, but not with so much insistency that anyone would notice. I bent often to pick up garbage and placed it on my sister's still form. She only shook slightly now in her hiding place, and the darkness did well to cover the fact that my burden required extra effort to push through the dirt and grass. The whine was gone from the wheels, and they often stuck in the turf, but I kept it moving.

I found a few articles of clothing that none of the other volunteers had yet gathered, so I put those over her along with other items to include crumpled paper, and even a few bricks that were lying in random locations around the field. I have no idea how long it took me to return to B, but it felt like an eternity. My heart raced in panic, and I was sweating despite the chill in the air, but I somehow kept enough composure to finally arrive at the border of B with Peska.

Most of the trucks had finally departed, no doubt taking the remaining members of Group A to (what would be obvious to me later) a sure death. Aside from a dusting of stars, we now stood in near complete darkness. We had all become silhouettes of real people.

"She's inside," I said, gesturing to the carriage. My father and sister Ester looked at me with incredulous stares, then down at my pile of debris. They didn't respond audibly, but I could see starlight reflect off the tears that welled beneath their eyes.

When he was sure the transports had left for good; my father had us clear off the items covering Peska and he pulled her from the carriage and into his embrace. Ester and I joined and we held each other in the silence of night. We didn't talk or cry. We just held each other for so long I cannot remember ever letting go.

IT WAS NOT until the next day we found out the truth about Group A. Somehow, the information leaked to us. I don't think the Nazis even cared to keep it a secret.

They all died. Each man, woman, and child was shipped from the soccer field to the gas chambers in Chelmno, Majdanek, and Treblinka. Group A had been wholly exterminated. Peska should have been among them. I was relieved only to know of her salvation, of the time I bought her…for in the long run, that was all it was. Those of us held in reserve in Group B were devastated. Many of the people in A were our friends. They were from the same neighborhood, attended temple at the same synagogue. Those people had been a part of our lives and had been torn more fluidly from our presence than even my mother and brother had been, as they had died slowly before our eyes. It was a stab into the heart of an already broken people.

Group B was not destined for the same fate, at least not right away; instead, they hauled us away in street cars to the ghetto in the city of Lodz, Poland. It wasn't far, but the city was larger and the rumor was that what had happened to us was happening all over Poland as the Nazis were consolidating their slave populations.

GHETTO LITZMANNSTADT

OUR NEW HOME, if you can call it that, was a far cry from the small confines of our pen in Pabianice. The Lodz ghetto was huge. Called Ghetto Litzmannstadt by the Nazis, the population of Jews here exceeded three hundred thousand people at one point. This was in part due to the fact the Nazis sent Jews from many cities and countries to Lodz—even from places like Germany, Austria, and Czechoslovakia.

Barbed wire surrounded the entire complex of buildings and every ten to twelve feet a tower stretched above the fences. The towers housed Nazi guards who manned their stations with submachine guns to make sure none of their prisoners would escape.

People tried—now and then.

They were shot for their efforts. But like moths to a flame, they kept coming. Gunshots became my nightmare and, despite their consistency, I never got used to the sound. Sometimes the Nazis shot Jews just for fun.

Litzmannstadt was the second largest ghetto during the Holocaust, only smaller than its counterpart in Warsaw. It became a factory for the German war machine, a veritable center for the industrial processes that would ultimately aid the endeavors of our Nazi occupiers. These factories included metal plants, fabric facilities, and other various essentials for the war effort.

Upon arrival, officials gave us our assignments. They sent me to a straw factory with my older sister. My job each day was to help in the manufacture of straw shoes Nazi soldiers would wear. The Nazis sent these shoes to the men who were fighting the Soviet Army along the Eastern Front. They used straw because it helped keep the soldiers' feet warm in the frigid northern temperatures. The work was boring and repetitive. But each day, I went to the factory, did what I was supposed to do, and then returned to my father and sisters in the one room we shared. Days became weeks became months, and the drone of my everyday existence was as much sustenance as bread and soup. Yes, the work was boring, but the repetition was necessary for survival then, an entity that I needed as much as food for my family. It gave me the impression there would be a tomorrow.

LITZMANNSTADT WAS TOTALLY isolated. Unlike the ghetto in Pabianice, here we had no contact at all with anyone non-Jew. The fences and police saw to that. The Nazis used local law enforcement to man the length of the fences twenty-four hours a day. The black market didn't exist in this isolation as it did in other places, so there was no extra food or other goods being traded to sustain life. People inside, instead, were trading away the last of their possessions and family heirlooms for an extra slice or two of bread. Gold for a day's extra meal.

Once again, our general daily ration was a single slice of bread and a bowl of watery soup. The difference came in timing; they gave us the soup at work. I was just as eager and happy to have my portion each day, but so many people went without. Those who were sick and too weak to work did not eat when they needed it the most. Others forced themselves despite their condition to find a way to work just so they could receive the second half of their daily ration. The Nazis conditioned us like dogs. We worked for food, and only ate if we did the job or task they trained us to do.

People died in Lodz in numbers that no one could have imagined in Pabianice. Tens of thousands died of starvation and disease. People *died* in the ghetto. But they were *killed* in the ghetto as well. Removed from the ghetto by the thousands, they went to their deaths or to serve as slave labor elsewhere. Although there was some amount of struggle to maintain culture in Litzmannstadt, the conditions were altogether harsh.

More than once the soldiers in Litzmannstadt organized mass transports of children to be sent to extermination camps. I was returning from work one day, eager to see my family, when I was stopped abruptly by a soldier. He placed an iron grip on my shoulder and shoved me forward with an order to move. There were other children already in tow. We all kept our heads down and did as we were told. The soldier marched us to the edge of the ghetto where there were other children waiting in large groups, boarding train cars in neat lines, looking over their shoulders for parents who weren't there. My group was edging closer, but we were still thirty or more yards removed from the cars that were filling quickly.

I didn't recognize any faces, so I looked over my shoulder like the rest. I hoped my father would be there, say something to the guard, then take my hand and lead me away. But it wasn't my father who saved me. It was a quota. The cars were full enough for that day and the soldiers told us to return to our homes. I wish they had really meant *home*. As we worked together often, Ester was aware I had gone off with the others. It was a pleasant surprise to my father and my sisters that I returned.

There aren't too many other stories to be shared or memories from our time there. Everything was the same. The same clothes. The same food. The same work. The same nightmares. For nearly two more years we survived in this horrible place. We remained in Ghetto Litzmannstadt until it was liquidated in the summer of 1944. At the time, there were fewer than sixty-eight thousand of us left, a far cry from the height of just over three hundred thousand.

NAZI AUTHORITIES INFORMED those remaining that Litzmannstadt would be emptied of all occupants, and in short time. In groups of five thousand, they had us report to the nearby railroad station. For the first month or so of this gradual and mechanical process, the trains took their occupants to the death camp in Chelmno. There, they were all murdered. My family was not among the earliest selections for transport, and Chelmno was eventually closed. Too close to Russian forces, that camp was nearly removed from existence as the Nazis hid their crimes. After a pause in our removal, the trains began to run again. We didn't know to be more afraid one day than the next. We didn't know the others left to go to their deaths at Chelmno. We assumed we were all just being moved—moved to our next camp, our next half-life in a place where we would know again the meaning of slavery and torture.

FINALLY, OUR TIME arrived. We were somehow blessed to have our family unit remain intact and I left with my father and two sisters to the station. Nazis there herded us into cattle cars and boxcars. We barely had standing room, and breathing became a chore in the mustiness of the packed cars. We couldn't even sit down. There was no privacy and no room to do much else than stand, pressed against a neighbor, idle in our wait to discover what would become of us. The soldiers did not give us food or water, and once a car was filled beyond its maximum capacity, the doors slammed shut and we were cut off from all knowledge of the world and our fate.

We didn't know our destination—only that we had to do what we were told or die.

We rode like this for two days in miserable conditions and worse psychological states. If we had to relieve ourselves, we did…again, without privacy. There was a large barrel of human waste in the middle of the car. I felt sorry for those who had to stand close, but we all took shifts as we pushed that way if the need arose, then pushed away after our turn. The Nazis wouldn't have treated actual cattle that poorly. We went hungry and the thirst was beyond bearable. People cried or whimpered, but most of us were reserved in our misery. We didn't realize it until later, but people actually died among us without us even knowing, the odor of their decomposing bodies disguised by the putrid stench of waste that floated in the hot air.

Brief and whispered conversations broke the monotony.

"Where are we going?" asked Ester. She was a ghost of the beautiful young woman she had been.

"We'll work, probably," said my father. I don't know how he did it, but he somehow refrained from any negativity during our entire experience in the Holocaust. He was a brave man and a good father.

The train kept moving until the end of our second day.

Auschwitz/Birkenau

OUR TRIP SEEMED to take far longer than the actual two days that transpired while we suffered on our feet in the reek of human waste twisting with the stench of old sweat and death. When the train stopped, we still weren't sure our trip was over; it seemed it would keep going, only to take a break here and there, before the soft rumble of the wheels on the track would begin again and continue as a drone that numbed our minds and bodies into complacency.

This time, however, the doors opened and the immediate rush of fresh air came as a shock to the system, something akin to an immediate change in temperature. The cleaner air that sucked into the car was foreign, but we relished it in a way only someone who has suffered this torture can understand. Other prisoners dressed in stripes opened the doors and ushered us out. All the while, Nazi officers screamed at us in German to disembark at once. Someone shoved me forward, but I maintained my poor grip on my father's arm. At least I would be with him for whatever waited for us outside the car.

When we stepped off the train, everything was a mass of bodies and shouting, dogs and gunshots. German men in uniform yelled commands while fellow prisoners gave instructions and led us to the correct lines.

"Line up! Five across! March forward!" they barked at us with a viciousness that can only be born of hatred.

Another voice boomed over the others. This particular Nazi soldier looked at us with fierce eyes that knew our fate, while a twisted smile curled his lips. His commands were simple and direct, "Men over here. Women over there." My sisters went one way, while my father and I managed to push through the sea of people to the line for the men.

The soldiers were meant to be understood and followed without question. If someone was too slow to comply, he or she was shot or struck with the butt of a soldier's gun. Prisoners who already worked at the camp would drag away the bodies like it was habit.

Those prisoners, called the Sonderkommando, were also there to greet us and translate instructions for those unable to comprehend the guttural and angry German we heard. Their true purpose, though, was to take away whatever remained of our personal belongings. We didn't have much. Nothing remained of the Adler family photos or heirlooms, no jewelry or clothing—just whatever we wore on our backs.

We thought there would be nothing left to take.

We were wrong.

As the prisoners wove among us, asking for anything we still had, they also spoke words that I'm sure saved some lives.

"Look strong," they whispered, "if you want to live. You've just arrived at the Auschwitz/Birkenau Extermination and Selection Camp."

We didn't know how to take the news. We had heard only rumors of this place and didn't know to fear it any more or less than any other. Our ignorance probably kept us from hysteria. A center and capitol for evil in the world, Auschwitz was the site of more murders than nearly anywhere or at any time in history.

Dr. Mengele and his henchmen were present to conduct their selection. I didn't know of his infamy then. Known as the Angel of Death, Dr. Mengele was an actual physician and SS officer. His reputation derived from two primary sources. He was responsible for many, if not most, of the selection processes when determining which of the incoming prisoners would go immediately to their death in the gas chambers and which would live. Also, he was the perpetrator of the vilest human experiments known to man.

The selection process was something to which I would grow accustomed for the duration of the Holocaust. The basic pattern included examination by Mengele himself or other Nazi officers. Those men would examine each prisoner in turn and decide if that person looked strong enough to perform labor—labor deemed necessary to the efforts of war. In Auschwitz, they had those deemed worthy of slavery ordered to the left. The rest—the young, sick, or old—moved to the right. They were the useless eaters. The Nazis killed people like those in the hundreds of thousands.

We saved Peska once, but this time was different. I had been able to protect her for a little over two years, but now I was helpless. My eyes followed her and Ester, ignoring much of what was happening around me. As soldiers and prisoners alike passed through my line of sight, I kept searching for her. Spotting her long blonde hair, I was able to track her through her line. She followed the other women through the selection process, pressed to Ester's side and pushed forward by the mob. She was crying and confused. When they made it to the front of the line, the soldiers split my sisters—Ester moved to the work line, Peska moved in the other direction.

My own selection came and went with little event; I was of age and healthy enough to serve the Nazis. My father was also passed through and we moved in the direction that saved our lives for the moment. All the while, my eyes followed Peska. I didn't know her fate yet, but the news would come soon.

Even from a distance, I could see tears streaming down her face. Other children and the elderly were her company as she moved in the opposite direction from my own group.

Peska turned one last time. We locked eyes, maybe thirty yards apart. Her blonde hair fell over her face as she twisted to see me. Her beautiful, full eyes should never have been consumed by that much fear. She turned back when the woman behind her pushed, and then they all moved on to the gas chambers.

AT SOME POINT after the war, I learned the truth. Those in the lines unable to work received orders to move toward buildings that housed what they were told were showers. There, they were told to remove all their clothing, losing the meager remnants of their dignity right before their deaths. Members of the Sonderkommando would then shave the heads of the victims and send them forward.

"Memorize your hook number," soldiers told them, luring them into a false sense of security—with the intimation they would return to their clothing. This was one last way to keep the sheep culled and prevent panic.

Next, they were herded into large rooms whose ceilings were decorated with a mass of shower heads. When enough people had been collected, the soldiers outside shut and barred the doors with a clank of metal on metal. No water came from the showers as it can be sure so many expected. Peska must have been so scared during those last few moments of her life.

I WONDER WHAT my sister was thinking. I wonder if someone held her hand.

INSTEAD OF WATER in which to bathe and quench a thirst that had lasted for so many days, the room instead filled with Zyklon-B gas. It only took minutes for the Nazis to kill everyone in the room. It was an assembly line of death. Other prisoners entered the room afterward to take the bodies to the crematorium to be burned.

ONLY LATER WOULD I discover that my older sister, Ester, was transported to Bergen-Belsen, the same concentration camp where Anne Frank died. That day was also the last time I saw Ester.

I WAS VERY sad, but also enveloped by the chaos that was Auschwitz. I watched as Nazi soldiers stole babies from the arms of screaming mothers. The selection process determined they could work, but their children were useless to the Nazis. They ignored the women's pleas as the men tore infants from the mothers' arms. Sometimes, in front of their very eyes, soldiers tossed the babies into the sky and shot them down like clay pigeons—as if it was daily target practice. I watched as bullets split flesh and spilled blood in front of hysterical mothers. Some of the women themselves were shot in their panic; they had nothing left and chose death over obedience. Perhaps others looked on and wondered if that was the better decision.

Those soldiers were the unabashed heroes of the Third Reich.

How ironic…a man who could commit such evil was simultaneously able to go home after a day's work and play with his own children, go to church and pray, kiss his wife, and then work and continue the same evil on the days, weeks, and months to follow.

It is impossible to comprehend this paradox.

DR. MENGELE'S EXPERIMENTS varied in all degrees save for the level of evil. He conducted experiments on twins, toyed with amputation, and tried to manually change victims' eye color. He dissected murdered children, shocked and sterilized young women, and used many young men for altitude tests in pressure chambers. Those were only a few of the tortures he conducted in his "laboratory", his demented quest to understand and perfect the ideal race by tormenting others.

I was fifteen when I arrived at Auschwitz/Birkenau. I was among a group of other boys my age whom Dr. Mengele selected for an unknown experiment. After the war, we found out those experimentations were altitude tests. The Germans needed to know how high a German pilot could fly without supporting breathing apparatuses and other equipment. Young Jewish men were the test subjects; guards forced them into chambers and Mengele and his cronies would adjust the pressure, watch the results, and take notes. Most often, the young men would die slow deaths in severe pain. Their eyes would pop out of their skulls and they would bleed from their ears—all before taking their last breaths.

That should have been my fate.

ON MY FIRST night in the camp, I went to the latrine, my stomach volatile and aching from hunger. I heard someone call my name, but didn't recognize the voice; it wasn't my father. I turned and realized the caller was a friend of his from Pabianice and Lodz. As I held my hands to my belly, he walked over and took me by the arm. He smelled of the cattle cars and his rough stubble looked like dirt on his face. In his stripes, he looked so much like everyone else, I almost didn't realize it was him.

"What barrack number are you in, Yacob?" he asked with all earnestness.

When I answered him, his eyes looked worried and his grip tightened on my arm.

"Not anymore," he said. "Children from those barracks are going to die. They belong to Mengele."

I was afraid, but didn't have time to respond or ask questions. What else could I do but return to my barrack and hope?

He let go of my arm and took me by the hand as if I was a lost child. He led me directly to my father's barracks. We had been split at the end of the selection process, but I'd had no doubt, for some reason, we would be reunited.

The routine in Birkenau that we learned quickly, at the other end of gun barrels, was to fall out in front of each barrack early every morning. There, soldiers counted us and we again went through another selection process. The SS would choose prisoners to be sent to various camps or work sites for labor.

When our barrack was counted, the number wasn't correct. There was one too many of us. I was the one. I was the reason for discord in Auschwitz that day. Out of thousands, I was the source.

"Whoever does not belong, step forward at once!" shouted the officer responsible for counting our group.

A firm hand on my shoulder and a brief whisper from my father told me not to move. I remained as still as I ever had and waited for my death, the first of several times during my stays in three camps.

Because I was absent from one barrack and included in the numbers of another, the guards decided to count each of the nearby barracks until they discovered the discrepancy. We stood in formation for hours, awaiting news. Our legs ached and, in our weakened state, we only wanted to sit or lay down.

Of course, this wasn't allowed. We swayed like individual blades of grass in the wind, but maintained our feet and didn't fall. A bullet would have been our reward. My father never said another word, and I followed suit. Guards shouted and prisoners looked to their left and right.

I barely kept myself from trembling in the fear I would soon be discovered and shot for this crime. But I didn't even blink. I stared at the stripes of the man in front of me, memorized the lines formed by the wrinkles in his lice-ridden scalp, and held my breath for minutes at time.

Finally, word came that a young boy was missing from another barrack…my barrack…where I should have been. There was some discussion that we couldn't hear, but ultimately we discovered the commanding officer that day had grown tired and didn't want to waste any more time searching for one person; the Nazis needed their slaves, after all. Time was money, and the war effort needed its backbone. He began walking up and down the rows of prisoners in our barrack, but didn't take long and never approached me. He randomly selected another young face and sent that boy in my place.

I am sure that boy died. I cannot take blame, but I feel so awful. Someone died in my place, a victim of Mengele's tests and trials. The German Air Force demanded to know the amount of pressure a body could withstand. The young man who went in my place most assuredly died horribly, his eardrums popping and eyes pushing slowly out of his head as the Angel of Death turned the knob one degree at a time.

These things went unpunished for so long and were not divulged to the world until the Nuremburg Trials after the war.

Had I died in his stead, I wonder if he would have survived, if it would have been him who arrived in America and had a family. I owe that boy these words.

WE ONLY REMAINED at Birkenau for ten days. Each day was a selection and work, counting and standing, little food and too much pain. At the end of those ten days, my father and I were part of a selection where Nazi officers decided we should be sent to another camp that needed laborers. We were sent to one of the eleven concentration camps in Kaufering, Germany.

I WOULD NOT return to Poland for sixty-seven years.

KAUFERING

THE TRAIN RIDE to Kaufering was much the same as it had been from Lodz to Auschwitz. Stifling and horrible. When I look back, it is surreal to think my expectations were so low I no longer cared to wish for anything better. Each day was as the next. Each day held a slice of bread, a bowl of soup, work, and the threat of death.

I arrived with my father in Kaufering in August of 1944. I would remain until the turn of the year.

Kaufering wasn't different in most respects. Our meals were the same; perhaps the soup was heartier there, with a few more added vegetables, but that was all.

Even though, by 1944, the Nazis were already losing the war, they had not given up hope of victory entirely and were still building camps. They built eleven new camps in Kaufering. They sent us first to Camp Number Four and later to Eleven.

The barracks in Four were quite small. We actually had to step down into it about three steps, and there was a walkway in the center with windows at the other end. Inside the barracks two shelves covered in straw would hold fifty people on either side, shoulder to shoulder and head to foot. The buildings were low and camouflaged with earth. In the interior of Germany, that was more important. They put grass and dirt on the only slightly slanted, V-shaped roofs. From above, the Allies might think it was only empty land and decide not to bomb the facilities and the free laborers the Nazis relied on so heavily to stay active in the war for as long as they did. It is a sad irony that the very Jews they wished to murder were the same men and women who worked the factories and sites that allowed much of the Nazi successes during the war.

The camp was small in comparison to Auschwitz or Birkenau. Each camp there accommodated approximately ten thousand prisoners or less.

EACH DAY, SOLDIERS woke us at five in the morning with shouts to clean and then line up in front of our barracks where we were counted without fail. Sometimes a man would be missing, and the guards handled the matter, but normally everything was like a well-oiled machine, exact and without fault. I've read books and seen films since that dramatize this process to certain degrees, but it was always the same. Always so formulaic. There were typically four sections of five hundred in our work group. The Nazi guards marched us out and brought us to our work sites. The march took about an hour and it was then we received the first half of our rations, our daily bread.

My father and I worked at an underground construction site, a hangar for Nazi aircraft, a place to remain hidden from the eyes of the Allies.

We did various tasks that aren't worth remembering—whatever we were told, whatever needed doing. The manual labor was long and arduous, and we weren't allowed to return to camp until about eight each night. There was never such a thing as no work to do, and we weren't allowed to rest or sleep during those hours.

At ten p.m., we were finally allowed to go to our barracks. There was never much talk, camaraderie, or worship of any kind. We were dead tired and slept through the night—when we weren't so sick or broken we couldn't shut our eyes for the pain. Those were easily the worst nights.

That was the first time I began to experience any true level of separation from my father. He wasn't always with me. Often we worked and slept in separate locations, and I began to grow accustomed to his absence. I lived for my slice of bread and thick cabbage soup. Some days I would imagine the lukewarm metal bowl that held my meal to be a fire. In the coldest days of winter, I would hold my face close to the steam that rose from the liquid and press my hands as hard as I could against the bowl's surface. I imagined the harder I pressed, the warmer I would become—that the fire would take away the chill and make me whole again.

ONE DAY I was assigned to work with a group of men which happened to include my father. I was happy to see him, but I kept my emotions hidden and didn't get overwhelmed with any sort of excitement. The soldiers that day told us we needed to move bags of cement from the rail to the construction site. This was among our most typical work. The bags were heavy and dusty and I choked all the while. Two of us carried one bag, but I was not paired with my father.

We weren't allowed to slow down from the prescribed pace. If we did, one overzealous Nazi guard brandished a brutal weapon that was almost more sickening than the gun he held in his holster. A broomstick with a thick, long nail driven through it became his baton. When we dragged, he struck us on any exposed skin he could find and then he would laugh through crooked teeth as we bled.

I must have been too slow. I struggled with what number bag I'll never remember. I felt the sting on the back of my neck before I realized what happened. The pain was fast and intense and I dropped to my knees in agony. I dropped the bag to my side and reached up for my neck. It was wet where I touched. The guard stood over me and threatened another blow in a language I was just beginning to understand without help.

Luckily, he growled some slur or another and continued down the line to find a new victim. My partner, a man I did not know, told me to get up and ignore the pain. As blood slid over my shoulder in a thin line, I got back to my feet, grabbing the bag of dry cement, and I continued to work. Some of the dust caked my wound and helped it to congeal. I was beyond tears that day. I would not cry in front of my father. I gritted my teeth and kept walking. For several hours more I carried the burden, the pain spreading down my spine like waves of liquid fire.

Later that night, when I finally returned to the barrack, I felt at the large, crusted scab on the back of my neck and fell asleep to images of the guard and his stick—laughing.

I still have a scar.

IN KAUFERING, OUR favorite times were during the air raids. The Nazis let us rest in hiding and turned off the electricity to hide traces of the camp's presence. We could breathe and relax, think and hope. Those moments were rare but welcome. I would even smile sometimes, crossing my hands over my chest while trying to conjure up a good memory from before the war. Sometimes it worked.

We knew little about how or why the bombs dropped and knew nothing of the progress of war or who was *winning*, if winning is even a term that is applicable in such cases. We had no access to any news—no newspapers or radio. We didn't even know the day or the time, more often than not. We were totally dehumanized.

SIX MONTHS AFTER we arrived in Kaufering, half of the prisoners of Four and Eleven (I'm sure the other camps as well) had either been killed or had died from mistreatment and malnutrition. Perhaps that is murder, too.

As they reorganized the camps, a Jewish Kapo separated me from my father and sent me to the concentration camp of Dachau. That day and that selection was the last time I would spend with my father.

Dachau

CLOSE TO MUNICH, Dachau was host to a vast array of people who were falsely imprisoned because of their race, creed, or cause. Not only did the Nazis put Jews into those horrible places, but in Dachau more than ninety percent of the prisoners were non-Jewish.

One could find every European nationality and other classification for man in Dachau—Germans who were political prisoners, gypsies, homosexuals, convicts, and Russian POWs. I was one of the small percentage of Jews. Work was not divided by race, creed, or political preference though, and I continued to work at the same construction site.

But I get ahead of myself.

LIKE I SAID, when I left Kaufering, half of the population of the eleven camps was dead. Luckily, when I departed, my father was not among those numbers. He was still alive. I was selected randomly one day to go to Dachau. As usual, the Nazi guards had us form lines. One officer (he wasn't distinct from the rest), walked up and down the lines at a leisurely stroll. He would point and order us in a rather calm voice—for one of his station—to move out of line and form ranks to his right. In this situation, you simply did what you were told; there were no other options.

He approached my row and I saw my father at the head of the line. We were separated by several men between us. I knew he would be selected, regardless of the cause. It was difficult to be optimistic in the camps, so I always assumed that each day could be the last I would see my father.

The officer glided right past him, pointing at the next man in line and continuing on. I didn't even have time to worry about myself, nor would I have had cause. One line was like the next.

But it would prove to be the day they would separate us.

The officer's finger pointed directly at me. Like a trained dog, I moved quickly to the right and joined the others. There was no look back, but I wonder now how long my father's eyes followed me as I walked out of Kaufering and out of his life.

Nazis, many with dogs on short leashes, surrounded us. And as was the pattern of marching here and marching there, we left Kaufering. I would never see the place again.

But I would see my father on several more occasions.

A FEW HOURS later, we arrived in Dachau.

Dachau was something of a parent camp. In some ways, perhaps indirectly at least, all the camps in that area of Germany (in and around the state of Bavaria) belonged under the jurisdiction of Dachau.

Life in Dachau was not much different than Kaufering, or elsewhere for that matter—save maybe for the absolute and large-scale death machine that was Auschwitz/Birkenau. We were all numbers, not names. We prisoners all looked out for each other as much as we could, but the reality is that this mattered so very little. We didn't become friends; we didn't learn names—maybe first names, but not usually. We didn't get acquainted. We talked; the adults talked. People who suggest much of anything otherwise exaggerated, fictionalized, or were the exception rather than the rule.

I was in Dachau from March of 1945 until April 27 of that year, merely existing. I had spent most of my time in enslavement in one of the various camps in Kaufering. The sleeping facilities there were different from Dachau. They had triple-high bunks without ladders, which meant they had to be scaled, and we each wanted to make sure we slept on the top. Sometimes people would relieve themselves in the bunk out of lack of options, so a spot at the top was prime real estate.

This life became routine.

Air raids were an occasional occurrence there as they had been in Kaufering. We appreciated them as we had there. The sirens would blast, screaming into the monotony of our day, and we were left alone as the Nazis and guards hid and kept us in our bunks. We could rest. Some of the old men wished the bombs would drop on us, put us out of our misery, but I enjoyed the moments to relax. They were the only times we were left alone except for sleep. It was waking rest, something most probably take for granted. I wouldn't allow myself to become party to the pessimism that dominated some of the conversation. I even heard one man praying in Yiddish for death.

My life was a routine of barracks, work, barracks, work. I didn't see the entire geography of the camp during my time there, and never saw the crematoria with my own eyes, but I occasionally saw the smoke. In Dachau, they didn't use the crematoria as often as in some other places. Men spoke about what happened there, but I put it out of mind. The purpose was obvious.

Later, when they took us out of the camp for the Death March, I remember seeing bodies piled in boxcars, headed for those very crematoria. The wheels of those carts turned with sickening squeals, a false mourning for the dead. Black smoke billowed in clouds of ash over the area as we departed, thick and unnatural against the sky.

I still can't understand or comprehend that systematic and mechanical approach to death. We are all temporary tenants of this earth. Why can't we just be good neighbors and try to make this a better world by helping each other and not hating? Hate created those piles of bodies. Hate lit the furnaces. Hate burned them.

I ENDED UP working at the very same construction site as I had during my time in Kaufering. The march to the construction site was longer, but from time to time I saw my father walking along on his own work detail. Sometimes his eyes were downcast or distant, as if he stared at something that no one else could see. At other times, our gazes would meet and it became the norm to wave at each other when we could. Those moments were like lifelines. There was some normalcy and a sense of safety in seeing my father. The world would go on and I would wake to another day, begin marching again, and wave to my father. Every time I saw his hand raise (that weathered, leathery hand), I had a sense that I could exhale and then inhale again more deeply than before.

Dachau was different from other camps in some respects, yet very similar in others. Indeed, the demographics were different than most, and other elements might have been different for this or that purpose, but it was still a place of forced labor and death. Over the gates into Dachau, like so many of the camps, the metal in the gate itself was formed to read, "ARBEIT MACHT FREI," or "Work sets you free".

The only freedom there was death.

Through those horrible bars was a large courtyard between the bunk houses on the left, where we were kept like cattle, and the Nazi officers' quarters and officiating buildings to the right. The entire property was surrounded by a shallow trench lined with barbed wire. More barbed wire topped tall fences on the other side. Not far away (it was a small camp compared to the likes of Auschwitz) were the crematorium and gas showers...the Brausebad. Ironically, not far from the camp's fences, German families lived in quaint, comfortable homes surrounded by a lush woodland.

Like everywhere else...more lines, more organization.

About every twenty-five prisoners or so had a Kapo, something like a foreman. A Kapo could be a Jewish person or some other type of prisoner. Many were murderers and other violent offenders lifted out of the German prison system and put in charge of groups of prisoners. It was the Kapo's responsibility to make sure that his group completed the work an officer assigned for a given day. One such officer at Dachau, the head of our camp, was an SS Obersturmbannführer—the U.S. Army equivalent of a lieutenant colonel. It was his job to oversee all the guards and laborers at the construction site. I wonder what it was like running something that resembled a construction company, but one whose workers were expendable to the point of death—feeding them little, working them from the rise of the sun until well past dark, and caring nothing for the psychological condition of the labor force.

ONE DAY, THE SS lieutenant colonel called my Kapo and asked for a young prisoner who could tend to his office on the construction site. I was given the job, which was much easier than my construction work had been. All I had to do was sweep the floor, dust the furniture, and clean up. It was starting to get cold around that time with the change of seasons, and he had a wood burning stove. I had to make sure the fire stayed lit. To be honest, it was almost a form of pleasure as I could at least stay warm for the hours I worked. When I first arrived every morning, I sat with my legs crossed on the office floor in front of the cold stove and opened it to clean the ashes. I would scoop and sweep out the charred remnants and black soot, disposing of the waste before loading it again with wood for his fire that day.

Not too long after beginning my tenure in this duty, I found something rather odd in the pile of ash. I reached for the object and discovered it was a block of some sort wrapped in dry wax paper, stained from the ash on one side. The lieutenant colonel was not in his room at the time, but I still glanced over my shoulder to see if anyone was watching. With trembling fingers I pulled the flaps of paper apart to reveal the contents. My eyes widened in utter surprise and I had to check over my shoulder again, sure I was doing something wrong.

A thin, dry piece of cooked bacon rested on a thick slice of white bread with a hard crust. I didn't look again. I was too hungry. I shoved the bacon and its congealed fat in my mouth and began to chew. It was tasty and had a rubber-like consistency. The flavor was instantaneous, and my stomach rumbled loudly for more every time I allowed myself to swallow a bit. The bread was quick to follow. It was wonderful, a rare happy moment in those dark years. Each bite was a smile, each swallow a laugh that no one could hear—the residual of optimistic hope inside my soul.

Almost every day thereafter I would find in his stove slices of bread, lengths of bacon, or some other delicacy for me wrapped in the same wax paper. He obviously put those things there for me to eat, or else he would have thrown them away. Was he something of an evil savior? I do not for a second believe every member of the Nazi party was an evil man or woman. I am left with the paradox of the situation. The lieutenant colonel helped run one of the many camps of death that nearly destroyed an entire culture.

But he also saved my life.

IN MARCH OF 1945, the Nazis finally allowed the International Red Cross to enter Dachau and distribute food sacks, which were like small care packages, to the non-Jewish prisoners. The Jews were dogs, after all and didn't deserve any aid. However, some of the non-Jews did have some food left over, and they gave it to the younger Jewish prisoners in what can only be perceived as true and honest kindness.

I received one of those food packages. I was lucky—if luck actually existed in a place like Dachau. I don't remember the man who handed me mine, but I was grateful. I clutched it to my chest and ran to my bunkhouse and to the area near where I normally slept. I immediately opened it, took out all of the contents and hid the food above my belt line. I hid it on my body so no one would steal any of it from me. Even though the Nazis did not tolerate prisoners hiding food, it still happened occasionally, and I am proud to say I was one of those perpetrators.

We marched to and from work in groups of five hundred (five across), guarded on the front, back, and sides by Nazi soldiers. The day after I received those leftovers, one of the Nazi guards approached me and asked if I was given a food package the day before. He looked the same as all the rest, nothing distinct, just symbolic hatred in uniform. It didn't even cross my mind to lie or try to hide any information from the man. I looked up at him and without hesitation said, "Yes, sir."

"Do you still have the sugar?" he asked. His accent was Ukrainian. They were almost worse than the German Nazis. Those men didn't get caught up in a national political movement like some Germans. Those men volunteered to leave their countries and work in this endeavor. The mean ones would rush us and the decent ones would let us go slower. We were rushing this time.

There was usually a small bag of sugar in the package—maybe a pound or a pound and a half. You see, you have to realize that at this point in March of 1945 Germany was at the tail end of an expensive war, and the country's own citizens, Nazi or not, were experiencing food shortages. One such shortage was sugar. So, it was not strange at all that the man asked me for mine.

"Yes, sir," I said.

He opened the duffel bag he was carrying over his shoulder and reached inside. I could only imagine what would emerge from the depths of the sack, but he merely took out a slice of semi-stale bread. It looked as good as anything else I had eaten in Dachau and I quickly forgot the sugar. He held it up to make sure I could see it.

"If you give me your sugar, every day I will give you a slice of bread like this," he said. I couldn't believe he was trying to make a deal with me. He could (if he had really wanted to) have simply taken the sugar and turned his back on me—never to speak to me again.

Did I have any choice? And what use was a pound of sugar to me other than to sweeten any bland item offered to me otherwise?

I gladly turned the sugar over to him because the bread was far more important. Can you imagine? An extra slice of bread a day as the essence of life?

The following day I made sure, as we marched to work, that I was on the outside of the line where he was guarding us and could see me. I wanted him to notice me and be reminded that he had said he would give me the slice of bread. It was probably the only time during the Holocaust I wanted a guard to single me out. After marching about twenty minutes, he passed by me.

I looked at him, and he at me, and he asked me in German, "What do you want?" His voice was rough with displeasure and he glared at me through eyes that held no concern for others. I thought maybe he didn't recognize me. I, of course, looked like all the others to some degree—we all had the same frail frame and the same shaved head. I was one of many.

So I told him, "I'm the one who gave you the sugar yesterday. You promised me a slice of bread every day."

"Here's your bread," he grunted at me in anger.

Instead of giving me bread, he took the rifle that he was carrying and hit me with the butt. It slammed into my rib cage with such force I immediately lost my breath as my vision blurred and filled with stars.

I collapsed.

Two other prisoners had to help me get to work that day, nearly carrying me to the site. I was barely able to function, the pain was so fierce. My eyes would frequently blind with tears as each jolt of pain coursed through my ribs and chest. When we arrived at the construction site, I almost couldn't make it to the lieutenant colonel's office. The first thing, as always, was to sit on the floor and clean out the wood-burning stove. This time, it was different; the pain made it harder and I grimaced as I fell to the floor and began my tasks. I was in so much pain. My rib cage felt like it was on fire. Breathing was nearly impossible as each inhale and exhale was like getting struck by lightning. I tried to remain strong, but could not help crying. My tears were obvious and streaked deep lines through the dirt on my face.

The lieutenant colonel walked up to me. It was the first time in five years someone like him, especially a high-ranking SS officer, had spoken to me like I was a human being—like I was worth speaking to in the first place. He was sitting behind his desk where he had been writing something and walked toward me.

"What's wrong, my boy?" he asked with a softness in his voice that I had before only heard from my father.

Even though I realized that the consequences of informing on a Nazi guard to his superior officer could be quite harsh, I was in so much pain I just didn't care anymore. I told the lieutenant colonel what had happened. To my surprise, he didn't become angry with me.

Instead, his voice softened more and he said, "Tonight, when we fall in, I want you to point out the man who made you this promise." The routine was that we had to line up each night to be counted, to assure no one was missing. The guards would stand right in front of us, rigid and stern.

Eventually, I left the office, returning to the lines that would take us to the camp with the others at the end of our work day. We formed our rows and I stood, trying not to hold my ribs, but instead keeping my hands at my side.

They began counting.

The lieutenant colonel had ordered me to point out the man who hit me. As the lieutenant colonel approached and nodded to me without a word, I froze for a moment. Reluctantly, I lifted my arm and with trepidation let my extended finger point to the promise-breaker.

Then I waited for my death.

I DID MY best to hide, making my way to the center of the five hundred prisoners, hoping to blend in and avoid the eyes of the soldier. Nothing happened. The next day was the same.

The day after that, hiding within the group, I almost forgot about the soldier and this new fear. But after some time marching, I looked to the fringe of our formation and caught sight of him, looking up and down the rows ahead of mine, his eyes resting on each wearied face of the destitute. He was apparently searching for someone and I knew it was me. I waited for the beating that I knew would ensue as surely as I knew I would always step one foot in front of the other while marching. Maybe this time would be it; maybe he would kill me. Nobody would do anything to him, not even the lieutenant colonel. After all, I wasn't even a real human being.

He finally spotted me and I nearly came to tears with the intensity of the fear. My ribs still hurt and were bruised badly in hues of dark purple and sickening yellow, but the pain was secondary to that fear.

He stepped into my row and approached me. I kept marching with the others, trying to look forward and ignore him while waiting with apprehension, fearing the worst. He came another step closer, then another. His hand rose as he came near me.

He handed me a slice of bread.

I couldn't believe what had just happened. I looked down at the bread as the soldier continued on his way without a word. I'm sure other prisoners were looking at me, but I didn't know them and didn't even waste my time to look up in my state of wonder. I started eating the bread, and somewhere on the inside (despite that my ribs screamed with each swallow), I smiled.

The next day (practically the moment I walked into the room), the lieutenant colonel spoke to me.

"Did he give you any bread today?" he asked in genuine concern.

"Yes, sir," was all I could say, still amazed this had actually happened, that I wasn't dead or beaten.

"Every day he is to give you a slice of bread as he promised. If he fails to do so even one day, let me know and I will deal with him." His eyes were serious and I could tell he meant it. He turned and walked back to his desk, sitting down and attending to the stack of paperwork before him. He didn't say another word. I began doing my chores in silence. But I was confused. Were all these men not evil?

Even though he was a high-ranking Nazi officer, in the earlier years of 1942-1944, he wouldn't have been brave enough to stick up for a Jewish boy over a Nazi guard concerning nothing more than a slice of bread. But it was near the end of the war—perhaps that was why he was no longer afraid to do the right thing. He was a decent human being caught up in the Nazi movement. This is hard for me, for many, to reconcile. But, I am sure this happened to many Germans. They didn't realize what they were getting into and, by the time they did, it was too late to get out. To argue or protest meant death as assuredly as one's Jewish heritage.

When the lieutenant colonel knew the war was coming to an end and he realized he could do something humane, he didn't hesitate to do so.

He saved my life. A Nazi officer saved my life. A gesture as simple as a piece of bacon wrapped in wax paper, and an order to a guard to keep a promise.

I wonder what happened to that man. Perhaps he was executed for crimes against humanity like so many of his peers when the Russians and the Americans got their hands on them. Maybe he fled to South America, as others did following the war… to hide in the jungles for the rest of their lives. Or maybe he was reabsorbed into the German populace, hiding all evidence of his former profession. I don't remember his name.

I will never know.

Had I the opportunity, I would not have hesitated to testify on his behalf. Imagine…a Jewish Holocaust survivor speaking up for a member of the SS.

WE REMAINED IN Dachau until April 27, 1945, when five groups of two thousand each marched out of the camp. It was called the "Death March". We were meant to die, one by one. We marched during the daylight hours, and at night we slept in the woods. It was April, and although it should have been warmer, it was still cold outside. Dressed in my thin, striped prisoner's uniform, I was cold and the chill went to the bone. To make matters worse, the soldiers took small groups of prisoners from each set of two thousand to the other side of the woods. I saw, on occasion, groups of those men led to their doom. They disappeared into the trees that were just beginning to wear their new leaves for the season. The green seemed dull, somehow.

The Nazi guards gave some of those prisoners shovels and ordered them to dig a long ditch. I imagine they knew they dug their own grave. Maybe if their humanity had not long ago been stripped, they would have protested, refused to dig and accepted their fate. We were slaves, little more than animals who obeyed without questioning at this point. They had no will not to dig, *not* to live those few more minutes while they stuck the shovel into the hard, cold, and crusted earth one miserable effort at a time.

When the ditches were complete, the guards ordered them to line up single file along the perimeter. They were shot to death, left to rot in the woods where people today, no doubt, walk their dogs and take weekend strolls. Our "stroll" was not over, though. Our long and arduous forced march held pains still, as yet, unrealized.

Hours passed like that; they were all the same.

During the trek toward Tegernsee, the Nazis shot anyone who no longer was able to continue the march. The need for rest was permanent. We were malnourished and many of us carried one disease or another. Dehydrated and exhausted, we had to move on. The Germans took turns riding in the trucks and other convoy vehicles. If a guard felt he had walked too long, he asked for reprieve and took a seat on one of the transports. We had to keep walking. It was walk or die.

I know I would not have survived another day. I don't say this to exaggerate the condition of the Death March or otherwise dramatize my situation. I would have died had I been forced to march just one more day. I was so very sick and the chore of placing one foot in front of the next was beyond painful. I was in a daze and couldn't tell you what I was thinking or feeling. I was nothing, reduced to a veritable walking corpse on the verge of falling for the last time.

I was not part of the group of prisoners the Nazis cut off from the back or from the sides that night in their effort to reduce the numbers and hide the evidence of their crimes. I curled up on the ground when we were allowed to stop. It was darker than most nights, and when my eyes slid shut, total blackness swallowed me. It was unusually quiet. I heard only the rasping breath of sick prisoners. No one spoke much; they were too tired.

I imagine it is very possible that I might have never opened my eyes again. If they had asked me to march again in the morning, my wake-up call would have been the heel of a Nazi boot followed by a machine gun bullet in my brain.

I fell into a deep sleep, free of nightmares and visions. It would be the last time I would fall asleep as a Nazi slave—the last night I fell asleep without my freedom.

WE WERE LIBERATED in the early morning on May 1, 1945, by the U.S. Third Army under General George S. Patton, and the U.S. Seventh Army under General Alexander Patch, both under the supreme command of General Dwight D. Eisenhower. Later, when I earned my citizenship in the United States, Ike was the first man to win my vote for the presidency.

There were less than four thousand of us left. Over six thousand men perished during those days, a horrible end to years spent in captivity. They had been so close to survival. Six thousand. That is still a simple fraction of what Hitler stole from Jewish and other cultures, but even one among them is too many.

That morning, there was a wet snow falling. It was so cold, but it reminded me I was alive and that, in itself, was shocking. I could hear adults mumbling softly to one another. That was against the rules the Nazis imposed; they wouldn't let us communicate like that. I tried to pick out pieces of conversations, but they were too hard to hear. However, the fact the adults even dared whisper to each other told me there was something wrong—or at least something different.

I tried to steal a few deep breaths, but it hurt. My chest ached and each intake of air was more of a chore than it should have been. Plus, the cold bit deep inside me; I could feel its teeth in my lungs.

I crawled over on raw elbows to some of the men I heard speaking and said, "What's going on?"

A middle-aged man with empty eyes like hollow spaces and haphazard patches of black facial hair on his cheeks spoke to me. "They're all gone. The killers. The SS. They're gone."

They had disappeared. The SS had left behind the regular German soldiers to watch over us. A few minutes later, tanks, jeeps, and trucks with soldiers pulled up with the white five-pointed star of the American Army. We didn't know who they were because the Russians had a similar insignia, only in red. I was young and, for so long, had been left ignorant of the world. It was different, but that star still reminded me of the Jewish star so many were forced to wear to mark them as dirty.

They spotted us. I doubt it was hard, thousands of broken men in various states and conditions, mostly prone on the ground, waiting for death.

An officer stood on the hood of one jeep. He had a bullhorn and spoke to us in a calming tone. His speech was simple. He said in an Americanized version of German, "Don't be afraid, this is the United States Army; you are all free."

That is how we knew our oppression had come to a close—that we were free. That was the moment. Someone had to tell us, otherwise we might not have believed. There was no happiness, just disbelief. From that day forward, I have been unable to express myself in any extreme form of happiness. The Nazis stole that from me. I learned to feel happiness within, without external expression.

I WAS ONLY SIXTEEN years old, the average age of an American high school student. I could barely stand.

Post Liberation

SOLDIERS PUT ME into an Army/Red Cross ambulance. So very weak, I was immediately hospitalized in a newly formed displaced persons' camp in Föhrenwald. When I was checked into the hospital I weighed sixty-five pounds. I was in and out of consciousness and could barely breathe through wheezing gasps. I was hospitalized for the first three months after my liberation. I had double pneumonia and was close to death.

One of the American servicemen who had helped put me into the ambulance spoke to me in a language I didn't know. He was sincere and hurt by the sight of us. He cried and, as the tears rolled down his cheeks, he placed a dirty palm on my forehead and let it rest there for a moment. With his other hand he reached up to give me something and his hand met mine. I took hold of the object and he let go, turned, and left. When I finally looked down, I saw that I held a leather belt with a shined metal buckle, a souvenir the U.S. soldier had collected from a dead German soldier. I looked carefully at the prize and saw in its center the bent arms of the swastika.

I have no family heirlooms from my boyhood. No possessions from the war—save one. I still have that buckle. Around the swastika is a raised inscription: "GOTT MIT UNS."

"God With Us."

One more day. One more day and I would have been dead. If I had contracted that illness in camp, I would have been allowed to die and then sent to the furnaces. Instead, I actually received excellent medical care, something that only hours before would have been denied to me.

I BEGAN THE slow process of becoming a human being again.

I was in a German hospital that had been turned into an institution for the well-being of the victims of the war. The doctors were international—a German, a Hungarian, and an American who all made the rounds. I remember I was very ill and burning with fever. German nurses had to dip sheets into ice water and alcohol and wrap my body to draw out the fever. Days passed that way, days of pain that were worse than my time spent in the camps, at least in terms of the physical suffering.

One of the days stood out more than others. That day some of the doctors and nurses were making their rounds. Our charts were at the foot of our beds. Some of them approached my bed and looked at the chart, shaking their heads and waving hands as if to say, *Not this one. He'll die soon, anyway.* I must have looked no better than a corpse. Their faces were grim to a degree, but it was with a normalcy that they had to conduct this business. I don't know numbers, but I am sure many people died in the hospital there, too far gone to be saved.

I said (unfortunately not out loud, but to myself), *Screw you. I'm not going to die now.* Not now. I was weak, but there was fight in me yet.

IT WAS A very organized and neat hospital. I wasn't in a private room (none of us were), but a small ward with about four beds. Everything was clean, white, and at right angles. There were others there with me, but I didn't speak to them or know what was wrong with them. They were ghosts at the edge of my vision, beings who experienced the same torment as I, but beings who weren't real to me then. Only the pain was real. I cried myself to sleep when I was conscious enough to feel anything.

But, like others, I recovered. And when I was better, I could talk, but I don't remember to whom or what about. Those days were like long, boring episodes of a bad television program. What had we to discuss? We didn't share our experiences in the Holocaust. Maybe we spoke about the weather, the doctors, or the food. I don't remember.

I WAS IN the hospital for ninety days. I was a skeleton when I arrived, but by the time I was released, I had put on some weight from fluids and food. I slowly began to regain my strength; it was like learning to live again after spending what felt like an eternity in a walking death as a soulless slave. First, I found my composure and ability to think clearly while bedridden. Then, I could move and talk. Finally, I took my first steps as a free man and left the bed, moving about the room and eventually outside of it. After a while I could move about in the main ward that was used for recreation. We patients played cards, checkers, and chess, anything to kill the time and feel like people again.

During my hospitalization, the International Red Cross along with the United Nations Relief and Rehabilitation Administration (UNRRA) conducted surveys of survivors across Europe and compiled lists of those individuals who survived. Those lists were posted in various displaced persons' camps like my own.

It was then I discovered I was the sole survivor of my immediate family of six and one of just five survivors in my extended family, which had numbered over eighty. I had held out hope that Ester or my father had somehow found a way to live, that I would see them again. The blow was harsh and quick as all hope was crushed from me. I couldn't find their names.

I LIVED IN the hospital within the camp from the time of my liberation until sometime around September of 1945. The camp itself then became my home and I lived there until November of 1946. I was seventeen when I left. That year or so was a blur as I rejoined something of a makeshift society. I didn't feel like I was home or that I belonged there, but I was safe and well-fed, and that was enough for someone who had been denied the basic requirements of humanity for so long.

MOST OF THOSE among us who were healthy enough to work did something to help the camp function. I worked for the woman who ran the camp, delivering mail and running other errands as she dictated. This gave me purpose and filled my time. Otherwise, at the Displaced Persons (DP) Camp, there was free food as well as room and board. We lived in barracks, but barracks that were a far cry from the ones in the concentration camps. Before the Allies had established the camp, German factory workers had used the space for their living quarters. Now, they were ours, if only temporarily. We had bunk beds and there were at least four of us to a room—a bit crowded for some tastes, but it was a paradise compared to our previous, cattle-like conditions.

THE DAYS PASSED (as they tend to), and I got used to the daily life in the DP camp. Some days I smiled, even. I was a young man on the verge of yet another life change, and to say there was no excitement in life at that point would be a lie. I was alive, after all, and there was assuredly some joy in that. I sometimes imagined what would happen next. Was going home an option? Around camp, people spoke of that often. Many of the adults talked of returning to their former lives, while younger people spoke of starting somewhere new, like Palestine or America.

I developed friendships, but nothing in terms of lifelong loyalties or remembrances. Our social skills had been stolen and, as much as we rejoiced in our freedom and the reclamation of our names, we still struggled (at least I did) with getting to truly know one another. However, there were others with whom I spent my time—working, playing games, or getting out of the camp when we could.

My first steps outside of the camp and into Germany, the country that bred the root of my captivity, were not without a measure of timidity and angst. I wondered what it might be like to interact with the countrymen of the Nazis. Would they hate those prisoners who survived and walked among them? Would I experience the same unjustified hatred because of my heritage that caused the death of nearly everyone in my family? Would anyone strike out against me? The answers, I found, were mixed.

On occasion, we walked or took busses to the small towns that surrounded the camp. One such town was Wolfratshausen, about two miles away from the camp. We would go there just to have something to do, to feel something different. The people there, for the most part, would leave us alone. They kept away and didn't bother us, knowing what we had gone through and the punishment the Allies had served upon the Nazis. It is possible they even felt some level of guilt, some notion that they had stood by while their fathers, sons, and brothers committed the worst acts in recorded history. They bore witness to it, yet did nothing. Of course, they had reasons—fear, the threat of death, and more. But the guilt must have been there, residing in their hearts. So, they usually just let us pass, without a word of greeting, friendship, remorse, or sorrow on their lips.

But not all experiences demonstrated those passive actions or neutral stances.

Some of the freed prisoners got involved in the black market. They were adults—men who had once known work and career and sought immediately to find that for themselves again. We lived in post-war Germany, a country that was bombed and indebted. Both former prisoners and citizens alike still had basic needs, needs that sometimes could not easily be met. Thus, black market trade was prevalent. I never took part in it, but I was aware it transpired and was often witness to it.

I was at the gates of the camp one afternoon, taking a break from running mail from office to office. I stood there in the warm afternoon sun and, for one of the first times, experienced a singular thought: I was comfortable—I felt good.

The mood would not last.

I saw one of the DP black market traders running from the German police toward the gates of the DP camp. I never found out if he was caught in some theft, or otherwise charged with anything. Who knew why he was running? But he ran and the police gave chase. He was on foot; they were in a car, swerving around a corner as the man bolted toward me and the interior of the camp. The pursuit continued, maybe for just a second, a millisecond, as they almost ran him down. Instead, the officer in the passenger seat drew a pistol and fired. On the spot—no questions asked, no reason given. Nothing. The man was dead not meters from me, blood pouring from the wound in his chest like a grotesque fountain. Maybe that man was a criminal, but he was shot like a dog, and I watched.

Maybe the war wasn't over. I was only a teenager at the time, but I had enough intellectual capacity to know what had happened was wrong and inspired by hatred. Their actions were a residual of the popular notion that Jews were not human and did not deserve humanity. Those men who drove down a Holocaust survivor and shot him deserved something. They deserved to go to prison for the remainder of their lives for such a horrible crime. But, it was no crime. Instead, they drove off with a squeal of tires, dust billowing up and over the body they left in their wake.

I stood quietly in shock; others realized what had happened and went over to the man's body. He was, of course, dead. I turned and walked back to the camp interior, unsure about my new world and the safety I imagined it held.

THERE WERE RELIGIOUS services at the DP camp, but I didn't attend. I had believed as a boy and was made to go to the synagogue, but I came to my own conclusions after the war, and the formal practice of religion was not among them. I am very proud of my heritage, but you see, being Jewish is a religious decision, not a race. I can become a Christian tomorrow and a Christian can become a Jew. And many of the world religions share the same basic concepts anyway.

I MADE SEVERAL friends in the camp. We would talk sometimes about what would happen to us after we left. Would we return home? Most of us knew that probably wouldn't be possible. We were still children and our families were dead. Not to mention our hometowns were still so full of anti-Semitism that a warm welcome would be unlikely. Without money or other means to start over, we had to look at other options.

Those options came at the DP camp. Organizers told us that there would be transportation and support services in various places around the world to help us get established, find us foster families, and put us in schools. The news was welcoming but intimidating. Starting over hadn't seemed a valid next step until then. We grew up in countries where we expected our futures to unfold. Then, during the Holocaust, we stopped imagining what a future might actually look like. While slaving through at twelve-hour work days for a bowl of soup and a thin slice of bread, thoughts of home, professions, and having children of our own weren't realistic. Pain was realistic. And hunger. And sorrow. All of my optimism and hope had been dedicated to seeing the next day, surviving a little longer.

Now, men and women with genuine kindness in their eyes told us to start thinking about our futures. For a people who were stripped of their fate by Nazi design, we had to imagine how to recreate that fate.

We all chose differently. Some of us went to the U.S., some went to Great Britain, and many went to other places in Europe. A large number of Jews went to Palestine after the war. Smaller groups attempted homecomings to their countries of birth with varying degrees of success.

Gradually they would send people out. Some older people just left, no doubt to find out what remained of their broken homes. They returned to places like Hungary and Poland where the hatred was still so fresh. How could you fault them? They wanted a return to their lives—lives that were full of possessions, families, land, jobs, and culture. Most would find the culture all but erased.

ONE DAY I walked into the office where I worked as a runner and there were sign-up sheets on the walls; attached to clipboards, they hung on nails and were written in different languages. Some I could read, others I could not. One such language was English, a woman told me. I read the names I could and the longest lists with the most names drew my eye first. She helped me decide, encouraging me toward a decision she thought best for me. As an orphan, she told me, I had more choices than many others.

Thus, I chose to go the United States.

With the woman's help, I filled out the required information—my name, country of birth, age, and other such details. It didn't take long and I didn't second guess my decision. It was the men from the United States who had restored to me my freedom; I couldn't think of another place I wanted to live.

The woman was in charge of the office for the DP camp, run by the UNRRA. I'll always remember her name: Mary Helen Cattel. She was from Santa Monica, California, and she told me that she had come to Europe as soon as she could when she learned of the things that were happening at the hands of such villains. She talked me into registering to go to the U.S., but didn't have to convince me at all. I was an easy sell.

"You are better off going to the U.S.," she said. "You will find a home and family there. We are a country dedicated to freedom, and you have more than earned yours. You can start a new life." She exuded kindness, and even her eyes were gentle. Blonde hair cascaded over slim shoulders and, even at forty or fifty, she seemed so young and beautiful.

I wish I could tell her thank you.

I filled out the application. With just the clothes they gave me, I was already packed and ready to leave.

WE WERE TOLD to meet at a local bus terminal. From there, we traveled to a waiting camp at a hotel in nearby Bremerhaven. Then we waited for the order to board a ship. From ambulance to a hospital and DP camp, then via bus and ship, I was on my way to America. When the ship arrived at Bremerhaven, we got on board. It was the SS Marine Marlin, a converted military vessel manned now by civilians. We numbered several thousand, of different nationalities, and for about ten days we sailed across seas and oceans of which I knew so very little.

I got seasick…one last tortured good-bye from the land of so many torments. I recovered quickly, though, and tried my best to leave those memories behind. For a while, they would haunt me in my dreams, but my ever-present optimism grew exponentially each day. I was a seventeen-year-old victim of war who had survived—and who was on his way to America.

On the ship, we passed time the best we could. We spoke about what the United States would be like. Some talked of Hollywood, others Ford and

Chevy. Tall buildings and baseball. The conversations were as various as our own backgrounds. When we didn't talk, we played cards or other games.

We also had freedom to move about the boat at our leisure. I saw the ocean and for days I could look in all directions and see no land. It was simultaneously overwhelming and exciting. For the most part, I had been deprived of the use of my five senses for any creative or free purpose. For years I smelled death. For years I saw hate cripple an entire community. For years I heard the cries and screams of the damned. But now I could breathe the fresh air without fear of a blow from a broomstick driven through with a nail. I could taste the saltwater on my lips and smile with the freedom of it all. It was truly an adventure of a sort, but I still had no home and no way to know what would happen to me next.

I worked on the ship in the mess hall, setting up the tables there with silverware, salt and pepper, and other necessities—things that hadn't been necessities for too long. It was easy work, but gave me purpose and took up some of my time during our voyage.

THE DAYS PASSED in relative comfort when one day the sailors told us we would see land in only a few hours. They were both right and wrong. We came close to land, but couldn't see it that well. We arrived outside of New York in the middle of a cloudy night. We couldn't make land as there was no one to take us once we left the ship, so we had to wait.

I walked up from below deck on a thin metal version of a staircase, my hand gliding up the rail in a firm grip, eager to see whatever I could. Maybe I thought I would see hills and flowing grasses, green with the reality of life. Instead, it was something far more amazing. The darkness of night only highlighted the glorious magnitude that was the city. I saw high-rises and lights beyond counting. It looked like a wall that rose beyond any ever built, riddled with holes and lit from the other side like a lantern. I was in awe.

I couldn't sleep that night, instead deciding to stay on the deck as long as they would let me. When I finally went back to my cot, I was restless and tossed in both exhilaration and anxiety. What would tomorrow hold?

EARLY IN THE morning when the sun was just peeking over the ocean at our backs, the man who ran the mess hall found me. He was gentle in all regards and shook my hand as he told me good luck. He reached into his trouser pockets and pulled out a wrinkled U.S. two-dollar bill. I was speechless. I reached to take the money and quickly put it in my own pocket. We smiled at one another and I finally managed to say thank you after an exaggerated pause.

American volunteers arrived as we docked and they took the orphaned children to a reception center in the Bronx. I was only seventeen, so I was still considered a child by most standards and so was included in that group. The volunteers were amicable and happy to help us in any way they could. Most, though they smiled, seemed burdened by a cloak of sorrow—it reminded me of someone who felt guilty for something. But for what should they have felt guilty? It was like a reverse empathy, a pity they felt for us but could not comprehend in full.

It was so overwhelming. They told us we would be matched with new families, that we would move to wonderful cities and towns all over the United States, and that we would be able to attend school and live long, happy lives. I can't remember if I believed them, but it was worth the risk of hope. I didn't want another family. I wanted my own, but I was mature enough to understand my parents and siblings were not being replaced.

I WAS IN the Bronx, for a little over a month. I went into the city whenever I could to explore the wonder that was my new environment. It was a busy place even then, and held more people, I imagined, than anywhere else in the world. There were so many cars, buildings, and people of different color and design that I was in shock during most of my excursions. It was wonderful to see the mélange of life in New York.

On New Year's Eve in 1946 our social workers took a small group of us into Times Square for the celebrations. There were so many people, and they all looked so happy. Men and women drank merrily in the streets. Bright-faced children screamed their excitement over vendors hawking trinkets and everyone was hugging and kissing at every opportunity. The commotion was contagious and I looked up with the rest as a globe of light descended from above, lit by what must have been thousands of bulbs, as people counted down in a language I couldn't understand. But the excitement and joy at the turn of a New Year and new life needed no translation.

I knew then America would really be my home.

I WOULD ALSO realize, however, that even in a place that seemed so wonderful, the disease of hate still could find hosts. We found out the next morning that a jaded man had shot his girlfriend or ex-wife in the crowd during the celebrations. He had somehow hidden a gun in a camera. It was a poignant reminder that hate could and would be everywhere. Hate was not a specific trait of one religion, one nation, or one man. It could traverse oceans and pass through cultural sieves like water. Unfortunately, hate is something all places and people have in common—at least in their capacity for it. Nestled in the heart of those thousands of cheering people was a seed of hatred.

Fortunately, the woman survived. Her survival, like mine, was a better reminder—one that suggested that hope and freedom from the oppressions of wickedness can prevail.

I COULDN'T SPEAK English yet, but I often went to Times Square by myself, and sometimes would visit an automat restaurant there. Those don't exist anymore, at least not to my knowledge. If I inserted twenty-five cents into a slot, I got a sandwich. It was all so modern and new—fun even. It was a nice change to have fun without worry. I went to movies with subtitles and, on the weekends, volunteers would take us on outings to parks and other attractions.

I carried with me the loss of my family, but still had room to enjoy myself.

I DIDN'T EXPERIENCE any racism or anti-Semitism in New York, but then again, I didn't have much exposure and couldn't speak the language. I don't know if I expected to hear the insults that came from the Poles and the Germans, but sometimes I imagined that when the people who walked by were talking, they were talking about me. I wouldn't have understood if they were being cruel or kind, but it still crossed my mind.

OUR SOCIAL WORKERS told us about foster families not long into 1947. It was like a strange version of a holiday, waiting to hear where we would go, who would become our new families. I wasn't as nervous as some; I had nothing to judge against save this inner-city experience. One city in America would be like any other, and I knew nothing of the country's geography.

One of the social workers, a middle-aged man with graying hair, told me that a family from Chicago wanted to take me in. I missed most of my world geography classes while in concentration camps and didn't know Chicago from Kookamunga. Furthermore, I didn't get much information about the family, so I was doubly worried. The man told me I would travel by train and he would send them photos of me so they would know what I looked like to welcome me. I calmed down at the realization there was good in the world, even if the good was outside my own cultural understanding.

I didn't ask many questions, only a few things about Chicago. Was it anything like New York City? Would there be others like me there? I didn't know what to ask or how to compare the newness of everything to my limited experiences.

A few days later, I was taken to a train station in New York. The last time I had been on a train, I was forced to stand in the worst conditions. This time, I sat, ate meals that left me satisfied, and slept when I wanted.

MY NEW SOCIAL WORKER, a Mr. Bob Danzig, met me in Chicago at one of the many rail stations in what proved to be another boisterous city—not on the scale of New York, but still impressive. This man took me to my foster family. Their name was Kohn. Simon and Beatrice. Simon was a German Jew and ran a men's clothing store. They weren't religious, so it was a good fit for me. They gave me my own bedroom (and a privacy I had never known) in a comfortable home and treated me with such kindness that it was a shock to my system. They gave me so much care, love, and understanding. I was like one of their own children, although theirs had already moved on to their adult lives.

We lived on the South Side of Chicago, and I would take the street-car into the city. My attempts at a new life actually began with a comforting remembrance of my old. I would travel to the West Side of Chicago, which housed the Jewish section. There I would get together with others around my age who had fled Europe before the war, or made their way to the U.S. during, or came later as survivors of the Holocaust.

Normalcy was our goal; we'd listen to music, dance, play cards, and otherwise socialize. I found that I could tell jokes, flirt with the girls, and be one of the guys. I discovered within myself the ability to forget, if only briefly, the horrible things that had happened to me.

But when I went to bed, the nightmares would return. Gunshots would wake me from a sweaty slumber and I could swear I heard screaming. Most people have nightmares about things imagined—about being chased, falling, aliens and monsters. My nightmares were real. They were a photo-graphic reimagining of Nazi tormentors, fierce guard dogs, and my sister Peska crying her way to the gas chambers.

SINCE MY FOSTER family was so giving and I was so inquisitive, they helped me get into classes to learn English. Most people in America were without a fluency in any other language, and communicating with people outside of my limited circle of friends was difficult. A local library held night classes for displaced persons, immigrants, and others. To be able to enroll in high school through the YMCA, I had to qualify, passing minimum requirements in read-ing, writing, and oral English. It was a good goal and focus, and it took me about a year to master the skills necessary to pass the exam.

The local Y had both night and day classes to expedite the educa-tion of those who were slightly older than the typical high school students at the public schools. Many of my classmates, in fact, were former soldiers, young men who never had a chance to finish their own educations before being shipped off to combat. They sat in desks alongside the young men and women they had helped to liberate.

To finish as quickly as possible, I took both available shifts and attended day and night school. I would take a bus to the Y and start classes at nine in the morning. I'd take a break to study or do homework in the afternoon at the same library where I learned to speak English. Then I would eat lunch, and would return to the Y to continue in my coursework until ten that night. This went on for two years.

It should be noted that prior to World War II the Y would not admit Jewish students.

HOWEVER FULL OF opportunities and freedoms, America was not without its own versions of anti-Semitism. I was in Ms. Foster's English class learning something about punctuation or spelling. She was exceptionally nice and looked after me in class. She didn't see how some of the others looked at me, though. Not everyone looked kindly on the new Jews in class.

Two boys followed me out of the room after I gathered my notebooks and went into the hallway.

They made sure to walk faster than me and passed me by without looking. Once they were a few paces ahead, they turned and looked at me with grins on their faces. They were both taller than me, and honestly a little intimidating, but nothing I could face in school at the Y could hold the same sort of trepidation I felt when looking down the barrel of a Nazi gun or being witness to death. I was proud of my strength in survival, even if I didn't know it yet, and stood my ground, meeting the boys with a look that told them I would not be afraid.

The taller of the two, a young man with short blond hair and the tired hands of someone used to manual labor, pointed a thick finger at my chest. With a smirk he said, "You must be the new Jewish student."

"Why?" I asked. "Do I look like Jesus?" Their eyes popped wide, and with a grin of my own, I walked around them. They didn't bother me after that.

I needed that moment of pleasure to deal with my next class. Mr. Franz was an ass. He mimicked my accent whenever I asked a question and was as mean as a rabid dog. But even he could do nothing to truly threaten me.

My terrors had been real, and no boy who thought I was different or teacher who made me the focus of his poor attempts at humor could affect me to the degree of my owned cursed memories. I smiled despite his taunts and bore the brunt of his class with the determination of someone who had already decided to make something out of a broken life.

AT THE END of those two years, when our dean, Mr. Wing, said my name at commencement, I rose to a splattering of polite applause, my eyes closing for only a moment to relish in the sound of my last name. Adler. The accomplishment attached to that sound gave me all the strength and courage I would need for the rest of my life. I was class president and the editor of our school newspaper; I was proud of what I had done.

I shook hands with Mr. Wing, and then traveled down the short line to receive the praise of the other teachers. Ms. Foster hugged me and I shook hands with most of the others. Another step brought me in front of Mr. Franz. It reminded me a bit of the selection process, standing under the scrutinizing eyes of judgment.

The thought was fleeting.

"It is because of you that I am here," I said and reached for his hand. He took mine in a weak grip and I walked off the platform and back to my seat.

There were two other Jewish survivors in my graduating groups. They took my hands in theirs and congratulated me as well. I looked at the program and saw their names under mine. Their last names were not their own, as they had been adopted by their foster families. But near the top in precise print, was the name Adler.

The Nazis took everything from me. They took my home, my family, and everything else that mattered to a young man coming into the world. But they could not take my name. I let others call me Jack, which was easier on the American tongue, but Adler would always remain a reminder of the family I had lost, of the family that came from Pabianice and had a proud history.

UPON GRADUATION, I entered Roosevelt University for one semester, and then attended the Walton School of Commerce (a business school). I planned to learn as much as I could to make a good living for myself and any future family of my own. Even then I knew I wanted my own family, my own children—it seemed the most logical way to start over after the loss of my own family. It would in no way be a replacement, simply a continuation.

Those plans were not stopped, just postponed, when in the 1950s the U.S. enacted a draft. Most young men of any wealth or of political relation found themselves exempt.

I was not. Instead, the government classified me as 1A—highly qualified for service. I could have exempted myself, for purposes of continued studies, but I saw the draft, not as an obstacle to freedom, but a means to protect it. I was eager and honored to serve the country that had won me my freedom from tyranny and oppression.

I never saw combat, but I was stationed at various bases within the United States during the Korean conflict. Since I had learned to type during my time at the Y and my brief experiences in commerce school, I became a clerk, assigned to tasks suitable to such a profession. I didn't raise a weapon or march into war, but I did my part seated behind a desk—one keystroke at a time.

In the interim of my studies in commerce school, I was able to take correspondence courses offered through the United States Armed Forces Institute through the University of Wisconsin. I found the discipline involved in the combination of work and studies an easy transition from all-day sessions at the Y and, worse, my time before liberation. Although monotonous, service offered another type of home and another sort of family.

As a member of the Army, I was granted the ability, through my various posts, to see and learn more about the country that had become my home. I was first stationed in Fort Eustis, Virginia, where I worked in the main office for the Transportation Corp of Engineers.

Oftentimes, I would take the bus into Norfolk when I had leave. On one such occasion, I was joined by a friend. He was a black man and like me was serving his country in the best way he knew how. Only due to lack of proximity and opportunity before, he was one of my first black friends. We sat next to one another on the bus, eager to see Norfolk and talking about all manner of things to pass the time. Racism and discrimination were not among those topics, but soon would be.

The bus came to a stop somewhere in the city, not far from the water. We were two young enlisted men, excited to have a good time and experience what we could of the world before returning to duty. After living in both New York and Chicago, Norfolk did not seem all that grand. It was deeper in the South than what I had experienced, and there were more people of color in Virginia. As such, 1950s-era segregation was immediately obvious.

We wanted to grab some lunch before walking around more, and entered one of the first restaurants we saw while walking along Granby Street.

The signs were clear. WHITE. COLORED. The large block letters appeared above arrows hand-painted blue that pointed to opposite sections of the eatery. My friend didn't say anything to me. He simply left my company and walked to the colored side, sat down, and ordered. He was used to the treatment; it was his version of normal. I was shocked, but followed suit, a waitress guiding me to the whites-only side where customers who shared the same skin color were eating sandwiches and chatting happily. Would they have felt differently if they had known I was Jewish? Was there a section for that?

No one else seemed to notice or care that a crime was being committed. That same friend was dressed in the same uniform and that same friend was serving in the same army. He and others like him were allowed to take up arms and fight for their country overseas, but if they wanted to be treated like equals, they were living in the wrong country.

It was hard thinking about and dealing with the absurd reality of one people's lack of freedom in a country that was built on the very principle. It would take over a decade more before blacks were treated like real people and true citizens.

After we ate, we left the restaurant in silence and I never asked him to clarify. I never asked why. I wish I had, but I think I was too sad.

I WAS NEXT stationed at the Valley Forge Army Hospital in Phoenixville, Pennsylvania. There I served as a clerk who prepared papers for soldiers being discharged. It was a humbling experience, meeting and working with service men who returned from abroad with any number of injuries and disabilities. One such man was the first quad amputee to pass through the hospital doors. Visualizing what he must have endured to fight for our freedom made me both sick and sad. More importantly, though, I was grateful.

I listened to their stories, and although my accent was noticeable, they never asked me for my own. I just told people I was from Europe and they left me alone. (For so long I kept my story to myself. Not until the late 1980s did I first begin to share. I didn't want people's pity or anything like that. I didn't regularly speak about my time in the Holocaust until 1992. I think reliving the pain was too hard at first and something to which I had to acclimate. I didn't want to talk about it and shut down when people became too curious, even later with my own children. I guess this is an obvious example of Post-Traumatic Stress Disorder. I remember once, seeing a book in my son's room about the Holocaust. I had mixed emotions concerning the discovery, but still refused to speak to him about my experiences for years more.)

My TIME IN the army was without any spectacular event. I worked and gave my remaining attention to my coursework. I was a private who spent his free time with new friends, sometimes traveling to Reading or Philadelphia. I began to live a bit more, and my nightmares became less frequent, almost non-existent. On Friday nights, the local Knights of Columbus hosted a dance in town. I joined the others, danced with girls, and smiled more than I had in years.

When I had served my due, a social worker helped me to find a place to live and I began my life as a civilian and citizen of the United States of America.

I MOVED BACK to Chicago (it was as much a home as any), but lived with another family from whom I rented a room. I took my first real, non-military job as a salesman for Mailing Brothers Shoes. I sold women's footwear and got paid seventy-five cents an hour plus one percent commission on my sales.

I never know what life might have in store for me, and I had never imagined I'd be doing something like that. It didn't last long. One day there was a sale that brought in a large crowd. A woman asked question after question, nagging me to no end, and tried on shoe after shoe. Finally, she asked if she could try on the shoe in the window display. I walked to the window, past it, then right out the front door. I never returned.

Sometimes you have to do that—know when to walk away, that is. Other times, you can't walk away, for one reason or another. Then, you have to persevere.

I didn't think women's shoes were worth my perseverance.

I took work next as a rep on the general sales floor at Mandel Bros. Department Store. I sold men's goods, appliances, and anything else I could. When I wasn't working, I made it a goal to finish college. I studied accounting and business administration at the Walton School of Commerce again, this time finishing my studies without interruption.

My life became something like a normal American's life. I almost forgot the horrible experiences that had defined so many years of my life. Although I carried memories of my family with me all the time, I thought less and less about the war and went days and weeks without nightmares, without daytime visions of death, and without the depression that coincided with thoughts and memories of the Holocaust.

By this time, filmmakers were already dabbling in documentaries and fiction alike, all dealing with various visions of World War II. I ignored them when I could, and bore the rest with a kind of resolute determination that had become the hallmark of my survival. None of the films or literature ever got it *all* right. Directors and authors couldn't capture the vicious threats of demented men, the terrible screams of frightened and dying children, or the misery that came with losing everything one loves. How can a moving image fully portray the heartache of losing a sister to the gas chamber?

I ignored the ensuing political diatribes—who was to blame outside of Germany, what more this country or that country could have done, or any conspiracy or theory. The war had been real enough the first time, and I wasn't ready to relive it.

I TOOK MY first full-time job as a cost accountant with Superior Concrete Accessories. My first day was Friday, March 13, 1953. As time passed and I became more familiar and friendly with my co-workers, they finally began to ask questions.

"Are you Jewish, Jack?"

"Were you in Germany during the war?"

"Did anyone you know die?"

Yes, yes, yes, I thought but never said. I tried to be polite, but I never really answered their questions. When I did, I was vague and left out the details that would make the memory more real in any retelling. I didn't want it to be real anymore. I was happy to conduct my business as an accountant, continue to attend night classes, and enjoy what was a good life and living in Chicago.

I NEVER WENT to temple for religious purposes, but a synagogue on the South Side of Chicago was home to weekly weekend dances. It was also a place to feel a silent comfort with a people with whom I shared both heritage and a twisted contemporary history. Every weekend, it was good enough to walk side-by-side with friends and attend a dance. It was also there I met my wife-to-be, Miriam. Both of us loved to dance.

We were married on June 14, 1953.

FROM THERE, MY life was rather good.

I bought my first car. It didn't last long and others were soon to follow. I stopped working for a company and began to work for myself. I went to night school to obtain my real estate broker's license and learned other trades, and eventually went into business on my own as a real estate broker, appraiser, and insurance broker. Miriam and I bought our first house in Skokie, Illinois. We moved in around Halloween of 1959. We had two children, a son Elliott and daughter Paula. (They both make me so proud, my Miracle Family. They both graduated from college. Elliott graduated from the University of Montana and went on to win two Emmys for his work in film and Paula got a degree in accounting from the University of Illinois and leads a wonderful life, ultimately marrying a well-known sportscaster. My children gave me grandchildren—three boys and girl.)

The American Dream was something that became my reality. I was living proof the cliché was more than possible and not something to which people could only aspire.

But, despite the numerous positives that continued to accumulate in both my personal and professional life, I felt an unrelenting tug to the experience that was my adolescence. I still didn't want to talk about those experiences, but simply being around others like myself brought a comfort that some wouldn't be able to comprehend. With the urge to do something about these feelings, I helped create a Holocaust survivors club in Chicago. We met regularly, but we didn't share our experiences.

We knew. That was enough.

I HAVE ALSO discovered over the years that humor helps a lot. In dealing with the worst humanity has to offer, it is important to smile—even in the darkest days. A friend was going through a terrible experience, persecuted for various reasons that need not be discussed. I spoke to him one day, unable to give advice, but hopeful to make him find humor even in his misery.

"There were two men walking in the desert," I began.

"The first man said to the other, 'We better get out of here; they're castrating all the camels.' The second man looked at him with bewildered eyes and asked, 'Why do we need to leave? We aren't camels.'"

"The second man said, 'First they castrate you, then you have to prove you aren't a camel,'" I finished and looked to my friend. He smiled and sat down with me, perhaps a little more comfortable with his situation than only moments before.

It seems simple, but the reassurance provided by a joke or smile can overcome so much. We could use more humor and laughter in the world. In recovering from my own terrors, I found myself in humor and enjoy sharing it with others.

AROUND 1992, I found another outlet and method in dealing with the experiences of my childhood. I traveled one day to a middle school in Colorado. I was with a friend from Chicago who spoke on the subject of war and the Holocaust. I listened to his speech and, although it was informative, it wasn't the most engaging thing I had ever heard or seen.

When he finished, many of the children raised their hands. He called them one at time and, even though they were so young, they asked thought-provoking questions that begged for more from my friend. They wanted details. They wanted answers.

He couldn't provide them, for he was not a survivor; but I found I could.

I haven't stopped since.

ALTHOUGH IT TOOK time for me to become a member of the community of Holocaust survivors who regularly share their experiences, I found a unique and wonderful comfort in telling the complete truth about what happened. It was also refreshing to interact with young people in such a way that hope was the dominant and overwhelming theme.

AS LONG AS people want to listen, I want to convey my message, a message of hope and a message that hate cannot only be fought, but eradicated.

I want to change a negative into a positive.

I hope these words do this very thing.

I want to change "hate" to "help".

PART III

WHAT NOW?

My Vision

I WANTED TO share my story, but not for all the same reasons that most share theirs. Yes, it is important to relive these experiences for people, especially the young, so we can all learn from history and work to improve the human condition. But I also wanted to write this to delve not only into the past, but to explore our present and our future.

My vision is a paradox. I see both grim circumstances that have the capacity to ruin us, and I see hope all around me. To leave you with a message of hope, I must first explore those more bitter emotions that I feel when trying to understand our world.

RELIGION

MOST ORGANIZED RELIGIONS operate under the umbrella of PPO: Pray, Pay, and Obey. This is not necessarily a bad thing. Of course someone needs to pay; a religion is an organization, after all, and these types of institutions need funding. Don't they? And prayer is not a bad thing. Medical science has proven the psychological benefit of things like prayer and meditation. Prayer is just a form of faith for most people, and I do not begrudge a man his faith. Even obedience has its place. Most popular religious groups have fairly reasonable rules. Rules against violence, rules against cruelty, rules against immorality. So, PPO isn't necessarily an evil.

God created man, and then man created evil. However, evil (historically speaking), has often been a byproduct of organized religion, though it does of course have other origins. There have been more wars, more violence, and more death that can be attributed to religion than any other single source, probably most other sources combined.

Just to examine a handful, one can look to major wars such as the Crusades, WWII, and even the American Civil War when rich landowners used the Bible to justify slavery. Also, religious dogma has proven to be a driving force in the recruiting and inspiring of the poor and lower castes to head into combat in the name of some god.

What better way to motivate people? Fight for God. God will protect you. You will find yourself in a better place if you fall. Who could say no?

BUT HOW CAN so many people be so willing to kill in the name of a deity? Most of the major world religions share the same God anyway, though he may go by a different name. Christians, Jews, and Muslims all share the same God and even some of the same holy ideals—namely that we are all the children of Abraham. These systems of faith also have similar structures for good vs. evil and basic kindness, at least as it is expressed in the various literatures.

However, religion, to most extents, is the most divisive force on the planet. Although the aforementioned faiths have so much in common, they have argued and fought for years over holy lands, righteousness, and validity. Even groups that operate under the same general religion—say Christianity—have so many varying denominations and branches that they argue over which group has it right, who follows the rules more closely, or who best has interpreted the word of God. They all want a piece of the power and control, a stake in the financial and political mechanics of the faith game.

And most members of most religions, if they prescribe to the obedience of their chosen faith, wholeheartedly believe that everyone who does not believe as they do will perish and suffer for eternity after they die. Can a just God be that cruel?

I see goodness in organized religion, too. Many are charitable. Many serve to allow a sense of belonging and community that cannot be found to the same degree in other places. I just hope that when a young man or a young woman makes a choice (if they are even allowed to have that choice) to be a part of such a system, he or she is doing so with an open mind and a loyalty to the faith to which they belong.

I've been alive for a long time, and I have learned much in my years. One thing I have learned is that all religions (at least those recognized throughout the world) preach goodness, and kindness, and love. I've also learned that so many are willing to ignore this when it suits them. They fall to revenge when they feel wronged, turn a blind eye when they see suffering, demonstrate indifference when injustices are obvious, and take to greed only too easily.

Some religions go as far as to develop terminology for outsiders, labeling others as infidels, pagans, and blasphemers—doomed forever. How can a religion do this? This is not religion, not a program of faith. This is a hate organization.

Religions preach the Golden Rule—that we should do unto others as we ourselves wish to have done to us, but so few practice what they preach. I might be pessimistic in my views on the systematic indoctrination of the masses that is organized religion, but I think that if there is a god, God, a prophet, or any other celestial being that gives us both purpose and reason, then that entity would be disappointed with the outcome that is humanity.

SINCE WORLD WAR II

OUR CRUELTIES AS a world nation did not cease with the eradication of Nazi forces at the end of World War II.

Some examples:

Even though I was liberated by men of all colors wearing the same uniforms and marching beneath the same American flag, when I arrived in my new home in 1946, I witnessed a kind of hatred as bad as that which certain groups harbored for the Jews. In America, black citizens were truly only half citizens. I witnessed decades of racism, forced segregation, and a civil war of sorts that saw a group of people of one color fighting so desperately for equality and rights on par with those of another color. Though I saw black soldiers (the first of their race I had ever really encountered) when the U.S. liberated the prisoners of Dachau walk alongside their white brothers, they were not equals.

Systematic and legalized racism continued after World War II in South Africa where it was a policy, not a choice. Called Apartheid, this policy was as evil as anything that happened anywhere else in the world. Granted, the fathers and grandfathers of its perpetrators were Nazi sympathizers themselves.

More hate spread in waves all over Africa. Things like genocide and forced conversions of lands and people have nearly destroyed an entire continent. Hunger and disease torment many of the countries that don't have the resources to combat these issues, while slavery and evil in other guises have helped make the continent of Africa a place of so many injustices.

All over the map, Communist countries deny people their freedom.

There are still slaves in our world.

More people die of malnutrition than from combat, yet nations spend billions in armaments and little (at least in comparison) to fight famine and disease.

September 11, 2001. The Nanking massacres. Genocide in Darfur. Genocide in Rwanda. Vietnam. Serbian ethnic cleansing. The killing fields of Cambodia. Christians massacring Muslims in Kosovo and Yugoslavia. Catholics killing Protestants and vice versa in Ireland. In the Middle East, the Israelis and Arabs have been killing one another since the formation of the State of Israel. War—war over gods, over land, over money, over oil.

Man, apparently, is his own worst enemy.

But there are solutions.

WE HAVE A United Nations, though I call it the Disunited Nations. If this organization did what its very existence suggests, what it was formed to do, they should issue a directive to all 193 members that no member nations will tolerate racism, bigotry, or hatred and won't teach hatred of others to their children. If they do, they will be expelled and be isolated politically and economically by all member nations, eliminating them from trade and other forms of commerce and aid. Why don't they do that? Y? The UN is supposed to unite us. Why don't they take steps to do so? Instead, the UN is a rather weak entity that allows its members to be led by greed, money, and lust for power. There are many member nations that are constantly at war with other nations, or in general people of other faiths; today, most of these nations are home to branches and sects of radical Islam.

They must act.

THE MEDIA SHOULD take part as well. If I had money to spare, I would advertise on TV and radio every half hour or hour and would use a few seconds to say, "Respect your fellow man." After all, the airwaves belong to the public. This idea of respect needs to be engrained in our souls. Most people and organizations don't do this, though, unless they want to advertise, run for office, or further an agenda.

MAN CAN PREVENT future Holocausts. The key is mutual respect guided by the Golden Rule. It seems so simple. If only people would just follow it.

My Return to Poland

AROUND THE TURN of the year in 2011, an organization called the March of the Living, International (MOTL) invited me to join them on their yearly trip to Poland. A truly international program, the MOTL gathers young people from all over the world to come together in both Poland and Israel to remember events of the Holocaust and to make the promise of *Never Again*.

I had to think long and hard about my participation and desire to attend; it was not an easy decision by any means. For sixty-seven years, I never harbored the wish to see Poland again. Yes, it was the place of my boyhood home, but it was also the same country that was witness to the death of so many people I knew and loved. The non-Jewish locals at the time of the German occupation (with some minor exceptions) did nothing to help my opinion of the place.

What was there to which I would return?

The answer came to me one day as I was speaking to a group of local high school students in the Denver area of Colorado. The children. Thousands of young people chose to go to Auschwitz and Israel over Cancun and other places of vacation, where undoubtedly a mass of their graduating friends would flock toward the end of the school year. These children were brave enough to venture from places all over the globe to bear witness to the remains of the destruction of six million Jewish victims, a million and a half Jewish children. These young people were full of courage and a curiosity I envied.

It was my duty to return to Poland. It was my duty to speak about my experiences. And it was my honor to join students in the endeavor.

I FLEW FROM Chicago to Warsaw.

The whole group of U.S. attendees were there coming in from Los Angeles; there were some other Holocaust survivors, staff, and psychologists. MOTL had a well-prepared and varied group, skilled men and women who could help with those children who took the experience to heart and who might have a hard time dealing with the emotional toll of what they would see and hear.

Most of the other Holocaust survivors had done this tour before, so they were accustomed to the troubles that might arise emotionally from the experience. I can't say I was. When the students cried, I cried; their emotions were my own as I walked through some of the worst places in history, head bent with the flood of memories. There was always a student there to take my arm and share the time with me.

THE TRIP MAINTAINED a rigorous pace and, from the airport, we went to the Warsaw Ghetto. Then we headed to Lodz. We went to the ghetto there and the preserved railroad station that took the prisoners to Auschwitz. There was also a preserved cattle car. It was like being in a museum of my own life, plaques and markers here and there, information to be had. And I had lived it all. It was not at all like the last time I had seen it. I closed my eyes and imagined being there with my father and sisters.

I can still see Peska so clearly.

It didn't take much to conjure up the vision of the ghetto in Lodz from my boyhood. Sixty-seven years it had been, but I could see Nazi guards walking the perimeter alongside Polish police forces as if they were ghosts in a dream. I could see masses of men, women, and children unloading in lines from the cattle cars, yellow Stars of David plastered to their clothing marking them as slaves.

I could hear my father's voice. "Stay close," he would say. "Do as you're told. We will be fine."

I was both sad and fondly reminiscent. Those mixed emotions would stay with me as we traveled to Pabianice, my hometown.

A LOCAL TV station met me there. They knew I was coming and wanted to interview me. There was a scholar with them, a man who maintained and studied statistics—a historian perhaps. He had a list of people who had lived and died in Pabianice during the Holocaust…he had done his research well and many of the names I knew. They held the interview in their broken English and my broken Polish, but communication wasn't a problem. They said I had no accent. That almost made me proud. For over sixty years I hadn't spoken a word of Polish, but it came back to me with little pain or effort.

We went to the cemetery. The dead in this place are the only Jews left in Pabianice. There, I had hoped to find something of my mother or brother. Aside from traveling with the students and making it a goal to share my experiences with them, I also had personal issues I wanted to address. I wanted to see the graves of my family. I wanted to look upon the last resting place of Peska in Birkenau. I wanted to see the home where I grew up. My home. So it was with that in mind that I approached the cemetery, surrounded by young men and women who all looked to me as I told them this was where my mother and older brother rested.

The place looked like hell. There didn't seem to have been an iota of maintenance. I learned that those who had died during the war had no markers. What might have been rudimentary reminders of their deaths had long since vanished due to rain and snow and the like. Sixty years. It was difficult; I couldn't find anyone there, though I looked for what seemed like so long. The students helped me, but to no avail. My mother and brother were still lost to time and history.

The pages of this book will serve as their tombstone, their names forever inscribed in the annals of literature that, along with others, serve to remember those horrible events.

Fella Adler.

Chaim Adler.

I loved them. I love them still. I remember them.

I COULDN'T FIND any graves that recorded any other names I recognized. All the remaining markers and tombstones were from before the war. There was one mass grave where the Nazis massacred a large number of local Jews. There was a little placard there saying what it was, but nothing else. The cemetery was macabre; I put flowers down on the mass grave, a small gesture of memory for those who passed.

THE GATES OF the cemetery were the most disturbing. They were covered with nasty, hate-filled graffiti—Stars of David with evil comments attached, swastikas, and other messages of hate. The people of Pabianice knew I was coming and didn't even bother painting over the graffiti. I asked them why they didn't paint over it. They had no answer.

But even as things like the gate and the missing markers served to inflict despair, it was once again those wonderful young people who helped vanquish it. They stormed the grounds of the cemetery, searching for Adlers. When they found one, they called me over with such fervor they might as well have been Adlers themselves. I went as quickly as my old legs could carry me, and although each of those moments was a failed attempt at locating my brother or mother, each was a successful and wonderful example of hope as demonstrated by the hearts of the students who stayed so faithfully by my side.

We then went into the city and stood upon the same main street I used to walk up and down as a child. To my astonishment, everything was still there—the ghetto and other buildings still stand. It brought back some happy memories, like functioning as a family unit in the city, but then it also brought back memories of the destruction of that family, of our lives and our culture. It was difficult to reconcile all my emotions, but I managed. I wanted so badly to visit the apartment building my grandfather had owned. I wanted to knock on what had been my own door and introduce myself. I imagined what I would say.

"Hello. I'm Yacob Adler. I used to live here with my family before the war."

I imagined the look of surprise that would cross the face of the man or woman who lived there, hoping they would let me look around and relive some of the happiest moments of my childhood. I did not get the chance, though. We had a mission and I was eager to take part. But it is a false memory that makes me smile. Maybe one day I will be able to do that. (My son did this very thing ten years ago and found the inhabitants there to be kind and warm to his questions and curiosities.)

We visited a restaurant in Lodz that served great Polish soup. They brought out a large kettle, full of potatoes and spinach. I could go on and on about some of the better memories that were resurrected by everything in Pabianice that evoked the senses. The smells and tastes brought me back to my childhood before the war, when my mother could still make things like that and when we had full bellies.

There was a certain kind of candy that I ate as a child. I remember buying it from the candy shop when I was young. When I found it on this trip, I bought all of it, a far cry from what I was able to do as a little boy. I shared it with the kids on the trip and it made me smile. To conjure happy memories from a place that holds so many negative ones is a blessing.

WE NEXT SAW the Pabianice Ghetto, a site that is now home to apartment buildings and businesses. They had not rebuilt the old synagogue. There is now only a plaque where it once stood. There is very little evidence of what transpired. Men and women live and work in the same rooms that became home to an overcrowded and starving Jewish population. It almost seemed surreal. Of course it happened. But it seemed so unlikely standing there.

This is why we have to remember. This is why we have to teach and listen and learn.

THE EVIDENCE LIES in the concentration camps. We visited one local camp where some six hundred thousand Jews were murdered. The camp was primarily intact because the villains who operated it ran so quickly—they were more afraid of the nearby Soviets than the U.S. forces and fled before they could erase all traces of their evil. At this camp, they took many children under two—they didn't just kill them, they tortured them. There was a mass grave and a signpost concerning those atrocities. It is still so unbelievable.

The students with me cried. Some of them took it very hard. Their faces were empty with disbelief. There was a historian with us from South Africa, a Mr. Ronnie Mink. Wherever we stopped, he told the students what happened there and you could see their expressions drop. He is a great lecturer.

WE WENT TO other concentration camps as well—like the one in Krakow. We went to Schindler's factory. Most of the kids had seen the film and the preserved factory was a poignant and profound marker for them. Then we visited one of the oldest synagogues in the area. Though the place held no true spiritual relevance for me, it did remind me of my culture and my people. It reminded me of the synagogue I had attended as a boy, the one Nazis converted to a stable before later burning it to the ground.

Our group traveled in five busses. We were a mass of people—kids, teachers, and other visitors and participants in the March of the Living. Each time we traveled by road, I would switch to a new bus and give a speech or talk to the kids, answering their questions. The other survivors did the same thing. The students' interest and tense, edge-of-their-seat attention reinforced for me the reason I want so desperately to share my story.

They cared. They not only wanted to know, they needed to know like they needed to breathe, and it was their contagious spirit I felt. It kept me talking, kept me answering their questions even when the worst of the sadness of memory was in my heart.

FINALLY, THE BUSSES stopped at Auschwitz and we walked to Birkenau. I was scared, to be honest. Although I hadn't spent much time there, it was my little sister Peska's death that plagued me the most, that stayed with me the longest when as a young man in America I twisted in my bed with night-mares. The remains of the gas chambers lay strewn about like so much rubble, the Nazis' poor attempt at erasing the evidence of their crimes—like no one would care to remember that millions died there.

I approached the debris holding a single yellow rose in memory of my baby sister. I trembled as I got closer to the rocks and concrete remnants of death. A light drizzle fell and gray clouds crept across the sky, increasing the melancholy of the moment, but serving as a stark and appropriate reminder of the sorrow the place holds. Peska took her last breath at that very spot, a breath full of poison and pain and fear.

I began to cry and gripped more tightly the black umbrella MOTL had provided me. I stood as close to the remains as possible and the group gathered around me. I don't know where I found the courage, but I began to speak.

"I arrived here with my father and two sisters; my baby sister was taken away to the gas chamber. And I can still see her face…" Tears began to overwhelm me as I brought the yellow rose up to my face and paused.

I bent to place the flower on the rocks and rubble at my feet. "…looking into her eyes…her saying, *'Help me'*." People around me took pictures and were respectfully silent, but they weren't there anymore anyway. I was with Peska, standing in line. The rain hit our faces, although in reality I held my umbrella. Each drop was a tear.

"But I've been wondering, for sixty-seven years… she must have been so frightened, being alone. I was wondering, hoping that maybe someone held onto her…" I said, beginning again to gather myself.

"The irony is that mankind embraces hatred must faster than respect for each other—for some reason. I don't know; I have no explanation for it." I stopped to wipe my face with a handkerchief, tears still welling in my eyes. I went on, "But maybe one day humanity will realize that we are all of one race, the human race, and that we should help each other, not hate each other." The simplicity of my own words struck me hard enough that I had to stop talking. There was a moment of silence, everyone respectful as they looked at me. We eventually moved on. I am not sure I could face that spot again, but I am glad I was there—glad I could stand in that place and remember.

THE FOLLOWING DAY WE explored more of Auschwitz at Birkenau. There were students there from all over the world. They were from England, France, Germany, Poland, Australia, the United States, Canada, and more—a truly global experience that, like the students themselves, filled me with hope for humanity's future.

You regain faith in humanity when you see kids from so many nations and creeds, when you see how they get along, when you see how they behave and how they care. It restored some of my own lost faith in the nature of humanity today.

I AM NOT sure I could go again, not sure that I could handle it. Some of these people, like the other survivors who were with us, have gone time and again. I just wanted to see these places and say good-bye to my family and a life I had once led. It was so difficult, although so worthwhile—an interesting and indescribable combination of emotions.

But it wasn't all sadness and dark clouds. My happiest moments during the trip were the exercises in positive psychology they had the kids perform for each other to keep spirits up despite the gloom of our historical excursions. They knew I was the jokester of the bunch and asked me to do five minutes of stand-up comedy. I agreed. I was happy to put smiles on their faces.

There was one doctor who came with us. He was a specialist in urology, although he attended as a general practitioner. I thought I would have a little fun. He was a really nice guy and didn't mind.

"Urologists are also called Moils—someone who does the circumcision. One such man wanted to build up his business so he opened up a front store. In the window on display, he placed a huge, decorative clock.

"After he opened, people asked, 'Do you fix clocks?' He said, 'No.' 'Well, then what do you do?' 'Well, I'm an urologist....a Moil.' 'Well, why then would you put a clock in the window?' 'Well, what would you like me to put there?'"

This got a few laughs, but might have gone over some heads, as the cliché goes.

The kids generally liked my comedy, or at least pretended to. I got a few other laughs when they called me to the stage; I was limping and looked to be in pretty bad pain. Someone asked what the matter was.

"I have a headache," I said. "How else would you know I have a headache if you didn't ask why I was limping?"

I have a different brand of humor.

I JUST ENJOYED being around the kids. We sometimes rode the bus two or three hours at a time and the kids would take turns sitting beside me. Some of their favorite questions were things such as, "How did you deal with it all without becoming suicidal?" I liked answering that question since there was purpose and care in my response.

I would tell them, "Even though all of us found ourselves in a hopeless situations, the one thing the Nazis couldn't take away was what was in our heads, and for survival purposes or techniques, you have to have a positive mental attitude. Very few who gave up hope survived. Suicide is a permanent solution to a temporary problem. I just dealt with what was happening to me. My positive mental attitude came from my family. I wanted to see them again."

I REMEMBER SOME of the kids specifically. One wonderful young student from Los Angeles was Sydney. She hovered near me, like a mother, to make sure I was okay. She was perhaps seventeen or eighteen years old and acted like she wanted to protect me and take care of me. I'll never forget her face— never forget their faces.

Like I've already mentioned, it is important to note that those students, instead of going to places like the Bahamas for vacation, spent nearly five thousand dollars to attend the two-week trip to Poland and Israel.

At one point, the woman who ran the trip told each of the young participants that their mothers had written them letters to read at a certain point on the trip. She added that some of their parents had to save for a long time, or even go into debt, to give their children this experience. They should thank them, she said. The students were in awe as she spoke and knew the meaning and love that came with this privilege.

The trip involved so many different people. Different places. But with all one goal: to never forget.

I WOKE UP on the morning of May 2, close to the end of our travels, and went to breakfast. Many of the student and adults were in deep discussion—it was obvious that something big had happened. Bin Laden had been killed, thanks to the heroics of the U.S. Navy Seal Team Six, as that Sunday, May 1st had come to an end. People were sharing the news, not with any excitement about a man dying, but with the energy and hope that comes with the elimination of a symbol of hatred. Here's some irony for you—the news of Hitler's suicide on April 30, 1945, was broadcast on the first of May. The news of Bin Laden's death was reported shortly after May first...

I was liberated on the first of May.

I like that day.

WHEN I RETURNED to the States, that group continued onto Israel. I got on my plane home, thoughtful and lost in memories, somewhat shut off to the world around me. The overwhelming nature of those experiences is still with me. I think about my return to Poland daily. The memories that stay with me the longest, those that I spend the most time with on a daily basis, are the memories of my time with the students, of their questions, of their concerns. They are the reason I went.

Unfortunately, I am not sure how much longer these types of experiences will be available to children of the world. There are now less than two hundred thousand Holocaust survivors. Most are in their eighties or nineties and live in Israel. I am one of the youngsters at eighty-three. I don't know of many survivors who are younger than me, and I am not getting any younger myself. In another generation or so, there will be none of us left to share. Thus, it is so important I share now.

I might just have to go back.

MY DREAM, IF an old man is still allowed to have one, would be that if I did return, I could do so with my family. If I could, I would pay for three generations of my Adler Miracle Family to visit the place where their family knew its roots—the place I'm from. I would take my time visiting those places where I spent so much time as a child. There would be no program, no need to do anything but think and feel, experience and remember.

Why I Speak

It is very important to open peoples' eyes to what hate can do when it turns to real evil, and I hope to speak as preventive education to teach others why they should not hate their fellow man.

I want to teach people that there are so many today who come to power and, once there, cannot let go. Rather, they become obsessed with power. But people want freedom. These two things clash and you end up with situations like those that have been seen with Hussein, and in more recent conflicts like those in Egypt and Libya and Syria.

I speak to so many schools and churches so I can advocate for stronger punishment on bullying. Not all bullies grow up to be evil hate mongers, but all hate mongers are bullies. Schools should not tolerate bullying.

The most dangerous bullies are those who have a religious or political following, because their followers don't question what the bully says—they just follow.

I speak because we need to teach mutual respect in schools. If there was mutual respect, there would be no hate. You don't have to love me or like me, just respect me as a fellow human being.

I think students should learn history, learn what happened and what is happening when there is no respect.

I speak because there are seven billion temporary tenants on this earth. One third identifies themselves as Christian. Over twenty percent are Muslim. One-fifth of one percent are those who have been bullied for thousands of years—the Jews. Even though they have experienced this for centuries, look at the contributions they have made to our civilization. I want students and people to whom I speak to know this. I want people to know that so many members of so many faiths fail to make their own contributions not because they are not capable, but because they focus on hate and not constructive and meaningful purpose.

I want people to know I don't speak out against faith, but radical and evil members of groups that operate under the title of religion. When I speak of radical Islam, I am not speaking of the predominant body of Muslim men and women who are good people. When I speak about certain occurrences in the history of Christianity or other religions, I still acknowledge that the average member is a good person. But those people are at times quiet. They should silence the voices of hate when radical members of their religions do horrible things—when they commit horrible crimes against humanity.

Silence accomplishes nothing when hate breeds so freely unchecked.

I SPEAK BECAUSE it is my duty.

In this duty, I hope to see the world change so as to show that man is becoming more tolerant of fellow man. I want to change lives. When I get a letter from a child that says I changed how she felt about things and now she respects people of difference more than she once did, I know I have had my part in making the world a better place.

I want to see the difference in humanity as humanity improves its own condition.

METAPHORIC REVENGE

I THINK THE ONLY final answer is to take revenge—not in the real sense of the word, as I am not a vengeful spirit, but something more metaphoric. We all must decide what that revenge will be. For me, I am doing my part. My family is my revenge, generations that Hitler and the Nazis could not kill. Speaking and sharing is my revenge. These words are my revenge.

THERE ARE NEARLY seven billion of us on Earth represented by every race, ethnicity, and religious group. This diversity should be a mark and measure of pride—we ought to embrace it rather than continually use it as a force of division. We can call it a revenge against hate and evil. Many nations today were built and continue to grow based on the idea of diversity. However, all over the world, hate groups plague us and threaten to tear the very fabric of peace.

Groups like the Ku Klux Klan and the Aryan Nation. Groups like the Nation of Islam and Skinheads. Or like Westboro Baptist Church. These are all the same. Our revenge—your revenge—should entail ensuring that these hate organizations become powerless and have no part in breaking the bonds of man.

Living in a society as beautifully diverse as ours, it would be nice if we all loved or even liked each other. We don't. And we don't have to—this is no necessity. The necessity is respect, and it is only through the mutual nature of this attribute that we can survive as the race of men. Mutual respect is the glue that bonds us in civility. For revenge against Hitler and future Hitlers (for there undoubtedly will be more), we should spread the cure of mutual respect like a vaccine against a disease. People will follow when good people lead.

But I am afraid.

I am afraid that unless humanity can learn and is willing to co-exist, we will gradually cease to exist.

Our revenge must be focused and immediate. It must be profound. No longer can the world find complacency in indifference and comfort while ignoring the worst in humanity. I use my words as a call to action, as a means to evoke change. I call upon you to be active in the fight against hate—to be a soldier in the struggle to free ourselves of this evil in all its forms and practices. Do not stand by when others suffer. Your revenge against the hate and evil in this world is to decide what you should do, then to do it.

I'm reminded of one of my heroes, Dr. Martin Luther King, Jr. He said that he dreamt about a time when men and women would not judge others by the color of their skin, but the content of their character. Our revenge should be to make this a principle and human law.

But for all of us, this revenge is best: don't bite the bait that leads to hate. Do not allow yourself to be a party to hatred in any word, intention, or action. Free yourself of prejudice, racism, bigotry, and other forms of hatred, and never treat anyone in any way that you yourself would not want to be treated.

I WOULD USE my last words and, some day, my last breaths to repeat these words, words that I share with you with all the hope I can muster:

Respect
Peace
The Golden Rule

PART IV

AFTERWORD

POSTSCRIPT

IN SHARING MY experiences with you, I also want to do something different. I want to provide the context for the atrocities that became the Holocaust. The Holocaust was the epitome and peak of a wave of anti-Semitism that flooded the world for thousands of years, an evil based on lies that have been perpetuated to this day. This is the context I want you to understand as you read my tale and others' tales.

I want to talk about the climate of hatred. I want to tell you about the historical happenings that are a series of tall columns, each collapsing into the other until the whole building falls and crumbles to dust. I want to share with you the world of hatred that was allowed to fester like an infection and become the Holocaust.

No child is born hating anyone. Hate is a learned experience. We learn it from our home and our social environment. When a child is raised in a hateful environment, he often accepts the teachings of that environment. Rarely will a young child ask, "Why hate someone who has never done anything to me?" It usually has to do with the target of hate being different-subscribing to a different religion, or being a member of a different race. I call these people who hate "bullies", and I use this word often.

As long as there has been a Jewish people, a Hebrew people, there has been anti-Semitism. Granted, the terminology for this systematic and often legalized form of the most extreme type of evil is a fairly modem invention, but the concept has been around for ages.

And despite what students all over the world learn in the limited nature of their history classes, many do not know the history of Judaism and anti-Semitism. They don't know they will find these prejudices and hatreds in places they would never expect.

In places like the Roman Catholic Church.

With people like Martin Luther, father of the Protestant Reformation.

Among respected world leaders like Franklin Delano Roosevelt.

In places like ancient and modern Africa.

In places just down the street from them, right around the corner... among people they know.

MANY DON'T WANT to know, and don't want to hear these things.

They must.

I WANT TO tell you these things. I want to build for you the structure that formed the climate of World War II and the most regulated and processed version of genocide the world has ever seen. Many think this started with the Nazis, but you have to travel back many years to learn when and how the Jewish people began to experience the hatred to which they have never allowed themselves to grow accustomed.

YOU HAVE NOW read my story, and yet I am only an infinitesimally small example of these crimes against humanity.

NOTES ON ANTI-SEMITISM: A BRIEF OVERVIEW

NOTE TO READERS: These historical notes are simply snapshots of important moments in history that have helped to form my own opinions and frame the events of my own life. Please see the end of the book for suggestions for further reading.

THE HEBREW PEOPLE can trace their heritage back over four thousand years. They thrived in areas of Africa and Arabia (among others) for generations that saw their inclusion in some of the earliest writings and civilizations. It was one of these civilizations that first demonstrated the willingness for men to hate, use, and abuse.

Considered by various religious texts to be the children of Abraham and Isaac, the Hebrews, to some degree, settled en masse in places like Egypt. There, they had their own "buttons torn", but to a degree far worse than I had experienced with a little boy one Sunday morning.

Finally, men and prophets among them found the strength to lead the people out of captivity and out of Egypt, establishing and beginning the earliest roots of the nation of Israel. For four hundred years, Hebrew people suffered—some to a more profound degree than others.

Their suffering was far from over.

SINCE THEN, IN places all over the world—but mostly in Europe—Jews have been expelled, burned, tortured, run into hiding, forced to convert to religions not their own, forced to give up their property, massacred, outlawed, banned from travel and business, attacked by mobs, taxed for their beliefs, forced to wear various symbols, drowned, gassed, stereotyped, and made to endure pogroms and the Holocaust.

In Europe, this legalized hatred was reinforced—to children and adults—by those they looked up to, including the church and state. So many at that time accepted it—that it was okay to hate certain people. And Adolf Hitler took it to the highest degree, preaching that those people had no right to live. After all, they were different.

During the last two millennia, Jews have experienced the worst humanity has had to offer. They are not alone; others have fallen to the same fate, but Jews are singular in the duration of their suffering. If one does the research, the reality of this persecution is obvious and consistent. Synagogue burnings all over the world. Forced conversion in places like Spain and Italy. Public displays of torture and burnings in countries with histories as proud as France and England. Do not let these facts escape you; hatred is and has been everywhere.

I DON'T MEAN to ignore or deemphasize the years of hatred that preceded what I address next. I simply want to focus on events and documented facts that stand out most to me.

IN 1492, KING Ferdinand and Queen Isabella of Spain ordered the people of the Jewish faith to convert to Christianity. If they didn't convert, they could be expelled from the country. This period was known as the Spanish Inquisition.

Jews and Muslims alike were forced to convert or flee; the Inquisition was a mandate dedicated to ensuring an orthodox Catholicism. As such, Jews numbering in the hundreds of thousands went to places like North Africa, Portugal, and Italy. There, they faced continued persecution and expulsion.

The Jews of Spain were no more; they had no identity and no home.

NOT LONG THEREAFTER, a man of religious vision based an entire doctrine on his hatred for Jews. In 1520 (and after his excommunication from the Catholic Church) Martin Luther, founder of the Lutheran Church, wrote the most hateful things about the people of the Jewish faith. His writings demonized, dehumanized, and stereotyped the Jewish people. He blamed them for all the ills in the world.

The very person responsible for the Protestant Reformation and translating the Bible for everyday man was also the very man who formally and publically vilified and demeaned those of one religion while promoting his own. In his text *On Jews and Their Lies*, Luther implied that Jews were people of the devil and advocated a theologically supported condemnation and attack on them.

I cannot imagine that there is a true man of God who could ever so willingly promote such actions of hatred. These types of men should not be deemed prophets, preachers, or speakers of any god. They should be called what they are: terrorists.

We all know something about Adolf Hitler, perhaps the most infamous leader in the history of the world. But not many know about his ties to Martin Luther. Adolf Hitler, prior to gaining power, was briefly imprisoned at the Landsberg am Lech prison in Germany where he wrote his book, *Mein Kampf*. His expression of hatred toward the Jewish people in that book was based on the writings of Martin Luther. Also, Joseph Goebbels, the Nazi propaganda minister, justified the Holocaust based on those same writings.

Luther was not the only man of the cloth to wrong the Jews. Certain religions and branches thereof made it an official practice. At times, the Catholic Church was among them. Prior to becoming pope, Pius XII was a Papal Nuncio from the Vatican to Germany, which is like being an ambassador. And when Adolf Hitler sought power in Germany, he and the future pope made an agreement of sorts.

The agreement was this: if the Rightest Party in Germany (which was the Catholic political party there) would vote for him, once he gained power Hitler would allow the Catholic Church to establish parochial schools throughout the country. And when the Papal Nuncio became Pope in 1939, and all during the Holocaust, not once did he denounce the atrocities that were being committed against the Jewish people.

Not only this, but when the war ended in 1945, many Nazi mass murderers were able to escape to South America by being provided false documentation. Their documents came from unlikely sources: the Vatican and the International Red Cross.

When the Jewish people were being slaughtered during the Holocaust—six million, a million and a half of whom were children—the world (for the most part) was sic, SIC.

Silent. Indifferent. Complacent. That includes our own nation, the United States of America. I see SIC everywhere. It's on the news every day.

In 1940, when the Catholic Church could have done something, they did nothing. Pope Pius XII was most assuredly SIC. He blatantly ignored repeated cries for help and once told a world leader to bear the horrible events of the world with patience. Like other leaders of nations and religious bodies of his time, Pius had the opportunity to act but chose inaction instead. Despite that, in 2007, the Roman Catholic Church raised Pius to the status of Venerable.

Authors and historians have since investigated the topic, taking sides and delving into the pages of history in search of answers. One such author is John Cornwell, a former Jesuit priest. His book, *Hitler's Pope: The Secret History of Pius XII*, is a telling account of the papacy during World War II. How I came across this book is an interesting story.

But, an aside first. In no way should my words be construed as an attack on the entirety of the Catholic Church. I simply believe that when individuals hide behind the guise of religion in order to advance an agenda, claim neutrality, or worse, then that man is wrong. Perhaps evil. There is today a form of radical Islam. They are nothing more than hate mongers. This is not an attack on the Muslim tradition; there are many good Muslim men and women, many good Catholic men and women. But when people wear their religion as a mask for evil, then it isn't a religion at all, it is an organization of hatred.

The man who gave me *Hitler's Pope* was, in fact, a monsignor at a Catholic school. I speak to tens of thousands of people each year. Many of them are students, spanning the country. Often, schools invite me to share my experiences and message, a message that calls for the abolition of hate.

Churches often call as well. I've spoken at both Lutheran and Catholic organizations. I went to one Catholic school where I was invited to spend the afternoon. After giving my speech to a respectful and curious audience, the monsignor pulled me aside and handed me the book. There was little explanation, but the gesture was obvious. The gift spoke to the fact that all men are capable of goodness, and all are capable of evil. Associating oneself with a certain religion, nation, or cultural practice does nothing to ensure morality.

Morality is something that comes from the inside, something that can be as common in a homeless pagan as it can be in a man of the cloth. The cloth guarantees nothing.

THESE ARE THE reasons I speak to thousands of students each year—because they represent the future of each nation, and they should know what happens if we tolerate racism and bigotry. It is up to them to make sure it never happens again to any group of people. Not ever again. I speak to them, to you, as an eyewitness to the darkest pages in human history. The Holocaust is the best—or maybe I should say the worst—example of man's inhumanity to man.

THE UNITED STATES of America may not be a perfect country by any account, but it's the greatest country in the world today.

But even my great nation of America has been party to inhumanity at times, not excluding World War II. Although it was the United States Army that liberated me, the country (like so many others) played host to anti-Semitism, neutrality, and its own notions of SIC.

I'm very proud to be an American. I became a citizen after the Holocaust and served my nation's military in both war and peace. However, during the Holocaust, when the United States could have saved innocent lives, they refused to do so.

When Mrs. Eleanor Roosevelt, the wife of then-President Franklin Delano Roosevelt, heard what was happening to the Jewish people in Europe under the Nazi occupation, she convinced the president to allow twenty-some thousand Jewish children to enter the United States.

Mrs. Roosevelt wanted her husband to show the world that the U.S. cared. However, President Roosevelt gave the assignment to a known anti-Semite in the Department of State. His name was Breckenridge Long. Mr. Long immediately told the various U.S. embassies in Europe not to do anything about it until he gave the go ahead. He never did.

All those children perished in the gas chambers.

Around the same time, a ship called the SS St. Louis sailed from Hamburg, Germany to Havana, Cuba. More than one thousand German Jews were aboard, crammed together in a desperate hope to save their own lives and find refuge. The Cuban government promised them they would be allowed to safely enter the country. The promise had been misleading. Upon arrival in Havana, only a handful left the ship under close supervision. Out of total desperation, the ship and the people sailed for the United States of America. Making land in Miami, Florida, the people on board pled with U.S. officials, explaining what was happening to the Jewish people under Nazi rule in Europe.

Their pleas and cries fell on deaf ears, and, having no other choice, the ship returned to Europe. Most of the Jews on board perished in the ensuing Holocaust.

IN MY OPINION, the most inexcusable act committed occurred when the United States and British Air Forces were bombing Germany and occupied countries around the clock—Germany and its occupied lands—in 1943 and 1944, up until the end of the war in 1945. They were bombing five miles outside of the Auschwitz/Birkenau extermination and selection camps, primarily targeting fuel depots. The allies were asked, even begged, to bomb the gas chambers in Birkenau, the crematorium, and the railroad tracks leading into Auschwitz/Birkenau. (Auschwitz was the concentration camp and Birkenau was the extermination and selection camp. They were within two miles of one another.) The request was taken under consideration by the

Assistant Secretary of State under Secretary of State Stimson. The assistant's name was John McCloy. After the request was made, McCloy came back a couple of days later stating, "I'm sorry we cannot help you, because we cannot divert the Air Force from their assignments."

Ironically, the allies once accidentally dropped a bomb into Auschwitz. If, as late as the beginning of 1944, the U.S. would have bombed just the railroad tracks more than a million innocent lives would have been saved. When McCloy's biographer asked where the order not to bomb Auschwitz/Birkenau came from, his answer was that it came from the White House.

ALSO DURING THIS time, there was a priest who spoke on a daily radio program out of Detroit. An anti-Semite to the core, the man preached hatred to and against the Jews throughout the 1930s. *They* were the reason for the Great Depression. *They* were the reason for the budding war. They were the reason for all the wrongs in the world. A religious man of the Roman Catholic faith, Father Charles Coughlin was among the first in his position of power to use the radio waves to spread any message.

How awful for the world that he used that pulpit and power for an agenda of evil.

Can we find it at all surprising that he spoke about his political support of Franklin Delano Roosevelt, or argued for the righteousness of the path of Adolf Hitler? Only with approaching imminent war did Roosevelt himself finally have to use his own power to cancel the Father's program.

In one of his broadcasts, Coughlin said, "When we get through with the Jews in America, they'll think the treatment they received in Germany was nothing."

OTHER ANTI-SEMITES from the United States might come as a shock to some.

Henry Ford, the famous auto maker, spoke against the Jewish people. Like Hitler, he agreed the Jews were a primary source for many of the problems in the world. He even sponsored literary projects such as articles and books; under his patronage, his anti-Semitic views spread through the United States. Many people don't know these things and only see Ford as a true American hero.

Joseph Kennedy was a military man and eventual ambassador to England. The father of President John F. Kennedy, Joseph was a worldly man whose colleagues were various other ambassadors including Herbert von Dirksen, the German ambassador to England. Dirksen and other colleagues (as well as a vast array of researchers since) have quoted Kennedy spouting his staunch opinions against the Jewish community, going as far as to say they got what they deserved in the Holocaust. One can conduct his or her own research and reach the same conclusions: despite a few well-placed Jewish "friends", Kennedy was an anti-Semite. It was a quality he shared with others of his time in similar positions of power and respect.

One such man was famed pilot Charles Lindbergh. Another touted American hero, Lindbergh was an outspoken member of a group that argued in 1939 that the United States should not enter into World War II on the English side. When war was ultimately declared, he did serve as a fighter pilot, but that does not discount the fact that in the 1930s he was a frequent visitor to Germany, and even received a medal from the government there. When the American Jewish community asked him to give up the medal, he refused to do so. He made a number of anti-Semitic remarks in speeches. Many vilified him as a Nazi sympathizer. Right or wrong, it at least begs the question of validation. We must always question. The truth of the matter lies in both the questions you ask and the evidence you discover.

There have been others—actors, athletes, politicians, and more. Men may have titles, but titles don't make men. It is with sadness in my heart that I admit that our world can still produce such evil. I ask that people only be aware of it and then stamp it out when they do experience it. Indifference to anti-Semitism is a proponent for the beliefs of anti-Semitism.

Ignoring hatred and evil *is* hatred and evil.

THERE IS A long history of hatred toward the Jewish people on behalf of the members of radical forms of Islam. A perfect example of this was the Grand Mufti of Jerusalem during World War II. His name was Haj Mohammed Effendi Amin al-Husseini. During the war, al-Husseini made an agreement with Adolf Hitler to provide manpower to help the Nazis fight the British. In return, he requested that Hitler's Final Solution (the mass killing of the Jewish people) be extended to the Middle East.

Al-Husseini lived up to his end of the bargain and provided the necessary support—men who fought alongside the Nazis to thwart the British. Though he lived in the heart of Berlin during much of the war, and he made such deals as the one mentioned, Al-Husseini tried to deny any knowledge that the Holocaust had even transpired—much like the president of Iran does today.

Now, there are new versions of this same type of hatred from this version of radical Islam. In 2011, a time that should be more civilized, there are organizations who brainwash their young followers to become suicide bombers. They tell them that, if they undertake such a mission, they will go straight to heaven and be met there by a prescribed number of virgins as a reward. A day hardly goes by when the news doesn't cover some event of Muslim extremist deaths by way of suicide bombing, be they Shiite or Sunni. And this—in the name of religion?

As a philosophy, radical Islam appears to have one goal…the destruction of Western civilization.

AS YOU CAN see, there is plenty of blame to go around.

The climate of hate and the climate of war that led to the Holocaust were not of singular make. The climate, instead, was a culmination of thousands of years of systematic, culturally learned and culturally accepted forms of hatred. This hatred took the form of racism, prejudice, stereotypes, persecution, bigotry, and more. Hitler and his followers were students of anti-Semitism. When they gained power, they became the executioners of an age.

It is important that we understand this context when regarding and reliving the experience of the individual in times of horror. For they, and I, are simply singular occurrences of the numerous who played witness. I am just one.

But if you can place my story into this framework, I know you'll have a better comprehension of the fact that I am but a brief illustration of the thousands of years and the millions of men, women, and children who were, like me, a victim of unspeakable crimes.

THE TWENTY-FIRST CENTURY

YOU MIGHT THINK that after all of these examples, people might learn something. But I ask you out of genuine concern: have we learned anything from our actions in the past? What have we learned?

So many men, women, and groups have found a home in hatred since World War II that it seems the horrid acts from that time meant nothing. Men like Louis Farrakhan. Men like Saddam Hussein. Men like Joseph Stalin. Using their power and the strength of those who followed them, people like these and others spread the disease of hatred.

Farrakhan hated Jews and others. He once said, "The Jews don't like Farrakhan, so they call me Hitler. Well, that's a good name. Hitler was a very great man."

Iranian president Mahmoud Ahmadinejad is a current world leader who has stated publicly on many occasions that Israel should be wiped off the map and the Holocaust was simply a myth—a myth perpetuated by Jewish people. Anyone who denies the Holocaust perpetuates evil.

If freedom loving nations allow Iran to obtain or construct weapons of mass destruction, Ahmadinejad and others like him will make Hitler look like a Boy Scout.

The Jewish people themselves are not free of hatred. No one group has a monopoly on what is good and what is evil. There are people who hate and who are capable of evil to be found all over the world, as members of every religion, race, and social group.

I could go on for ages, but one does not need to dig deep into the news of the last sixty or seventy years to find countless illustrations of the points I have made. We still find ways to hate. We find hate easier than love and fall victim to the potential for hate. We must refrain from these choices. I have not lost hope, but I am also a realist. Here we are in the second decade of the new millennium, and what have we learned?

I DON'T MUCH care about possessions anymore. I am eighty-three and realize fully that our time on this earth is fleeting and brief. But it would be interesting if I still had the buttons from my childhood coat. How symbolic they would be. I can see them in my hand, still marred by the dust from the ground where they fell. Each torn button, a moment of hatred held in my palm. The top button—perhaps the Inquisition or the Jews of Egypt. The next—the complacency to which so many held firm in times of pain and suffering.

I'D HOLD THEM tight and vow...I will not bite the bait that leads to hate.

ABOUT THE AUTHORS

JACK ADLER was born in Pabianice, Poland on February 1, 1929. His life changed abruptly in September, 1939 when the Nazis marched into his hometown and, in the years to follow, murdered his entire immediate family. One of less than two hundred thousand survivors alive at the time of this publication, Jack's words have reached over a million listeners as he travels and speaks throughout America and, recently, across the globe. He shares his story with students of all ages, churches, military groups, and any other organization that will hear his message. He currently resides in Colorado and is a proud father and grandfather of his Miracle Family.

W.F. ASPENWALL is an author and amateur historian. He lives in the mountains of Colorado with his family where he breeds dogs, hikes, and otherwise enjoys nature. An avid world traveler and part-time philosopher, he likes to share his adventures and experiences with various cultures through his prose. Author of many articles, reviews, and other short pieces, "Y" (co-written with Jack Adler) is his first full-length work. He is currently working on another full-length project called *The Chain*, a contemporary, anthropological-cultural study revealing wisdom through portraits of unorthodox individuals.

ACKNOWLEDGMENTS

FROM MR. ADLER:

I would like to thank my wonderful children, Elliott and Paula, and my four super grandchildren who gave a meaning to my life. I know I wasn't always perfect; I'm sorry and I hope that you'll forgive me. To my life partner Judy, thank you for all your love!

I also wish to thank Ms. Newman, who invited me to MOTL, and her staff who made the experience so wonderful. I must give thanks to a great man from South Africa, Mr. Mink. I want to thank all the schools where I was invited to speak and to the students who were so eager to listen. In this respect, a special thanks to Frances Pilch of the United States Air Force Academy and Florence Wagner of East High School in Denver.

I wish to extend a message of thanks to all the fighting men and women who serve in the military; I have been honored to speak to and with many of you at bases all over the country.

Finally, I have to thank the publishing team at Mbedzi to include Mr. Aspenwall, Karen, Elizabeth, Morgan, and Jacqui for helping my story become a book I can hold and that I can pass on when I am gone. You have helped me realize a dream.

From Mr. Aspenwall:

First and foremost, thank you, Mr. Adler. Thank you for sharing your story with the world. And thank you for allowing me to participate in this project. I am honored and humbled. Thank you for your patience while working with me and for your understanding in all matters. I respect and envy your compassion and concern for humanity.

I next need to thank the staff at Mbedzi Publishing. Karen, you make dreams come true and you give voice to the aspiring. It is your efforts, organization, and time that have helped Jack's message find a page. Elizabeth, your efforts in editing do not go unnoticed. You work miracles with a pen and for this, we thank you. Also, to Jacqui with the design and formatting, and to Morgan for the amazing cover and down to the wire assistance.

And my personal thanks go to my family…V., A., N., and L. I could do none of this without you. I love you.

Thanks as well to Dan, Priscilla, and Steve—Dylan, Cherry, and Robert.

Lastly, to my pre-readers…that team of daring individuals who braved the rough, unedited version of this book to give me your edits and inputs. Mike and family, your support in everything has been a life-saving kindness. Brian, you are my primary source of backboard feedback and a great friend. Jim and Molly, you are my heroes.

Notes and Suggested Reading

John Cornwell, *Hitler's Pope: The Secret History of Pius XII* (New York: Penguin Viking, 1999).

Tom Segev, *The Life and Legends: Simon Wiesenthal* (New York: Doubleday, 2010).

Phyllis Goldstein, *A Convenient Hatred: The History of Anti-Semitism by Phyllis Goldstein* (Massachusetts: Facing History and Ourselves, 2011).

Anthony Julius, *Trials of Diaspora: A History of Anti-Semitism in England* (New York: Oxford University Press, 2010).

Robert S. Wistrich, *A Lethal Obsession: Anti-Semitism from Antiquity to the Global Jihad* (New York: Random House, 2010).

Daniel Blatman, *The Death Marches: The Final Phase of Nazi Genocide* (Belknap Press of Harvard University Press, 2010).

Vivian Spitz, *Doctors from Hell: The Horrific Account of Nazi Experiments on Humans* (Colorado: Sentient Publications, 2005).

Leon Goldensohn, *The Nuremberg Interviews* (New York: Vintage, 2005).

Anne Frank, *The Diary of a Young Girl* (New York: Doubleday & Company, 1952).

Hamburg Institute for Social Research, *The German Army and Genocide: Crimes against War Prisoners, Jews, and Other Civilians in the East, 1939-1944* (New York: The New Press, 1999).

DR. MIKLOS NYISZLI, *Auschwitz: A Doctor's Eyewitness Account* (New York: Arcade Publishing, 1993).

SAUL FRIEDLÄNDER, *Nazi Germany and the Jews* (New York: HarperCollins, 1997, 2007).

ADOLF HITLER, *Mien Kampf* (first published 1939).

GERHARD FALK, *The Jew in Christian Theology: Martin Luther's Anti-Jewish Vom Schem Hamphoras, Previously Unpublished in English, and Other Milestones in Church Doc* (New York: McFarland and Company, 1992).

ERIC W. GRITSCH, *Martin Luther's Anti-Semitism: Against His Better Judgment* (Michigan: Wm. B. Eerdmans Publishing Company, 2012).

MARTIN LUTHER, *The Jews and Their Lies* (West Virginia: Liberty Bell Publications, 2004).

LEONARD DINNERSTEIN, *Anti-Semitism in America* (New York: Oxford University Press, 1995).

RAYMOND P. SCHEINDLIN, *A Short History of the Jewish People: From Legendary Times to Modern Statehood* (New York: Oxford University Press, 2000).

Notes and Suggested Reading Continued

Websites:

http://www.facing.org

http://www.jackadler.com

http://www.ushmm.org/

http://www.hmh.org/

http://www.motl.org/

http://www.history.ac.uk/ihr/Focus/Holocaust/websites.html

http://www.holocaustchronicle.org/

http://www.mchekc.org/resources/recommended_websites.aspx

http://www.jewishvirtuallibrary.org/

http://www.iranholocaustdenial.com/

http://www.oprah.com/oprahsbookclub/Holocaust-Resources-Museums-and-Organizations

http://www.museumoftolerance.com/

http://www.yadvashem.org/

CPSIA information can be obtained at www.ICGtesting.com
Printed in the USA
BVOW041226220412

288238BV00001B/1/P

Index